Civil War Ghosts & Legends

NANCY ROBERTS

BARNES
&NOBLE
BOOKS
NEW YORK

Originally published as *Civil War Ghost Stories and Legends*

Copyright © 1992 by the University of South Carolina

This edition published by Barnes & Noble, Inc.,
by arrangement with the University of South Carolina Press

1996 Barnes & Noble Books

ISBN 0-76070-366-3

Printed and bound in the United States of America

00 M 9 8 7 6

FG

Contents

Contents

Preface

My writing career might never have begun had it not been for the encouragement of writer Carl Sandburg. During his years at Flat Rock, North Carolina, Mr. Sandburg sent me a message saying that he liked a series of ghost stories I was writing for the *Charlotte Observer.* He suggested that they be published in a book. Such heady encouragement led to my writing twenty-one books, the latest this book of Civil War ghost stories and legends.

Sometimes I think it would make life more comfortable—give me a handy stereotype to fall into—if I could say that I am a Southern writer or a Northern one, but I cannot. Born in Wisconsin of parents who were North Carolinians, I believe, however, that I regard the Civil War from a relatively impartial point of view.

My father was employed by a chemical company not far from Milwaukee. For more than a decade I lived on the shores of Lake Michigan and thought of myself as a Wisconsinite. Later I lived in New Jersey and Delaware, and it was not until my father's retirement that I moved to North Carolina to join my parents at our family home in Maxton.

I was always aware of my father's love for history. Driving south from Wisconsin we seldom passed a battlefield without touring it, and so I saw many beautiful sites, including Gettysburg, where fifty thousand men died. My eyes grew moist when dad would read aloud the Union and Confederate losses. Staring at soldiers' faces

Preface

on the frieze of the North Carolina memorial there, I thought of my great-grandfather, Captain Fleming of Raleigh. Had he been among the Carolinians who had fought at this bloodbath on Pennsylvania soil?

I sometimes recall a story, told me in my childhood, of how, in the last months of her pregnancy, Emma Walpole McRae, my great-grandmother, fled Huntsville, Alabama, on horseback just before Federal troops arrived. Her discomfort must have been great on that long ride to North Carolina. "Miss Emma," as she was later called, left her home behind forever. I traced with my fingers the engraved name "Walpole" on a worn gray marble doorstep—all that remained of the antebellum house.

Emma Walpole McRae's baby boy, born in eastern North Carolina, was my grandfather. During my childhood years I knew him as the one who presided over the twilight depths of an immense general store fragrant with the odors of hoop cheese, country hams, seeds and fertilizer. The shelves were laden with bolts of fabric and black patent Mary Janes and over the front of the store a sign bore the name McRae Company in tall antique gold letters.

Men like John Sumter McRae were called time merchants. When I moved down from the North in my twenties, the words "Fall Terms" painted on brick store buildings puzzled me. I watched farmers come in to receive their seeds in the spring, and I saw them return to pay for them in the fall when their tobacco and cotton had been harvested and sold. I had no understanding of the important part merchants like my grandfather played in easing the postwar struggles of the Southern farmer until years later when I read William J. Cash's classic book, *The Mind of the South*.

Preface

The first stirring of industry in this section of the country that theretofore had produced only raw materials was the textile mill. The agrarian South had learned a bitter lesson. A society producing raw materials would always be at the mercy of an industrialized one.

As I grew up, I lived in two worlds. Winter months were spent among bustling Midwesterners, summer months in the company of my Southern friends, as I tried to slow my own energetic ways to fit their more leisurely pace. I am now aware that the emotional threads of the Civil War and Reconstruction period were still part of the climate around me in eastern North Carolina. They were woven into the South's view of itself and the rest of the country. Less than a century had passed since the War. The long summer days I spent in North Carolina during the 1940s and 1950s were still a time of transition.

As I wrote the stories in this volume the distance between the present and the war narrowed, and I began to realize that the war *really wasn't that long ago!* In the 1950s you could shake the hand of a soldier who had fought in the Civil War. Many readers of this book, or their parents, can remember that time.

Sometimes tears ran down my cheeks as I wrote and grieved for the men who died on both sides. Who can assess the loss to a nation of so many lives? It seemed that the human tragedy and waste of this war might have happened yesterday. I hope that these stories may bring the War Between the States as close for the reader as they did for me.

Nancy Roberts

Johnson's Island—
    This three-hundred-acre island, with a view of Canada on one side and Ohio on the other, was selected as the site to build a prison for Confederate soldiers. It was a frigid, forbidding prospect during the winter months. As one Southerner remarked, "It was just the place to convert visitors to the theological belief of the Norwegians that Hell has torments of cold instead of heat." It became a prison for officers, and among the well-known prisoners there was Major General Isaac Trimble, who had lost a leg in Pickett's charge at Gettysburg; Colonel Charles H. Olmstead, the defender of Fort Pulaski; and Brigadier General J. W. Frazier. During the forty months the prison with its flimsy, temporary buildings was in operation the number of prisoners varied from ten thousand to fifteen thousand men. It was designed for one thousand men. The officer in charge was Lieutenant Colonel William S. Pierson.
    Johnson's Island is three miles out in Lake Erie north of the city of Sandusky and a half mile south of the Marblehead Peninsula.

○○○

IT ALWAYS COMES AT DARK . . .

Johnson's Island, Ohio

An icy wind raked Joe's face as the small ferry plowed across the waves of Lake Erie. He and the others who gathered at the rail were all experienced quarrymen. The boat would leave Sandusky with them each morning and then return at dusk to bring them back. The pay was good for their work at the quarry on Johnson's Island—worth the boat trip out there, he guessed.

    Joe Santos remembered the first time he saw the island and how grim the old blockhouse had looked. Like a solitary sentry it stood, he thought. The building had

Johnson's Island, Ohio

been built to hold Rebel prisoners more than a century ago during the War Between the States—a war that didn't mean anything to this young Italian who had been in the United States only five years.

If he had acted on his gut feelings, Joe Santos might not have gone back after the first day—but there was the money; he needed it too much. There was something both sad and eerie about the island.

Had a history briefing come with the job, the quarrymen would have known something about what this place was like over a century ago. Here fifteen thousand men, prisoners of war, spent cold, monotonous hours, worked, sang, got sick—some never seeing the South again. As an icy wind whistled through the spaces between the single pine boards of the barrack walls, Southern officers shivered in bitter weather to which they were unaccustomed, prayed to be exchanged, and spent hours thinking of how they might escape. There was no easy way. According to a report at the end of the war, during the years of imprisonment only twelve men ever escaped from this island. Compared with other Union prisons Johnson's Island had a security record that was hard to match.

With the first heavy white flurries excited Southerners who knew little about snow engaged in snowball battles. By October crusts of ice were forming in Lake Erie, and the harsh, long Northern winter had begun. Soon the lake was solid ice covered by a white field of snow, and the island's ideal natural security became obvious to the Confederates. They were separated from the nearest point of mainland by a half mile of Lake Erie in the summer, and even in June and July the water temperature was not that of any Southern lake.

One Christmas Eve when the island was not heavily

It Always Comes at Dark . . .

guarded a small, brash group of Confederates stole away under the black, murky sky of a moonless night. They held no aces in this game with death, and there were only two cards they could play. One was to walk toward the mainland in the direction of Sandusky, Ohio, which meant back into the hands of the enemy. The other was to strike out across the ice toward Canada—many Canadians were Southern sympathizers—across thirty miles of trackless frozen lake. Survival chances were slim in the freezing weather, and their comrades at the prison never learned whether the Confederates who set out that Christmas Eve lived or died.

More than escapes, the prison authorities feared possible organized revolts with the help of sympathetic Canadians. The post commandant Major Pierson wrote to Adjutant General Lorenzo Thomas: "There was no dissatisfaction with their treatment which creates this disposition, but it is the result of the restless spirit of a set of very bad rebels." Well, what could you expect of rebels anyway!

Perhaps their "restless spirit" came from the fact that the prisoners in the camp were sometimes fired upon, according to a report of Confederate general Trimble. His account appears valid, for prison records mention the wounding by sentries of a number of Confederates and the killing of several. The shooting seemed to be connected with two rules: no visits between wards after 9:00 P.M. and all lights out by 10:00 P.M. On one occasion a lieutenant, hearing retreat sounded, started to his room, and a sentinel fired upon and killed him. On other occasions drunken sentinels fired between weatherboards at lighted candles in the wards.

Winter was not easy to survive in the Northern prison

Johnson's Island, Ohio

camps. It was a time of pneumonia and fever on Johnson's Island. The gray ranks were thinning each day, for medical attention was scant, rations of food were pitifully small, and there was only one blanket to a man in weather below freezing. Drainage on the island was poor, and with thousands of men eating, washing, drinking water, and defecating into holes on a small limestone island, the danger of disease grew greater daily.

Reports of inadequate rations for Federal prisoners at Southern prison camps aroused anger and a desire to take it out on Confederate prisoners in the North. When the South had food, prisoners ate. When the people and the troops did not, prisoners suffered also. It was impossible for Northerners to realize that both Confederate troops and private citizens in the South were beginning to suffer a severe deprivation of food from the widespread destruction of their crops and the scorched-earth policy of Federal armies. But in revenge, food rations at Johnson's Island were cut as they were at many other Northern prisons for Confederate soldiers, and thin faces with staring eyes and emaciated bodies struggled to keep alive. Soldiers who died were buried on the island. It was only raw courage and grit that kept men going month after month.

Once Joe Santos stumbled into a hole that had been dug more than a century ago, and he found human bones in it. He didn't explore much after that. He just worked the quarry and sat with the others at lunch eating his submarine sandwich of provolone, salami, and peppers.

The jagged cliffs of Johnson's Island jutted from the sapphire-blue waters of the bay, and the statue of the Confederate soldier stood forever clutching his musket

It Always Comes at Dark . . .

and gazing toward Canada. When Joe first saw it he thought bitterly of statues at home, particularly of the proud Il Duce, and he stood staring up at this one, puzzled. It did not have the arrogant features that dominated his childhood memories. He remembered the Italian leader's face from the past with mingled admiration and hatred—hate because of a war that had devastated his city and cost the lives of his parents. He had grown up fending for himself on the streets of Salerno. He knew he was lucky to be here and be able to earn a living as he glanced down at his strong, calloused hands. He guessed all countries had wars.

The start of them was filled with glory and excitement. He remembered the grand words the men had shouted, how proud he had been of his father in his fine uniform. But as the years passed many people had scarcely enough to eat, much less to feed any prisoners from the armies of the Allies. While his pick struck the gray rock of the quarry he remembered how sure he had been that his father would come home someday and go back to work in the vineyards, but his father had never seen the long rows of heavily laden grape vines again. And it wasn't because he hadn't wanted to. His mother had told him that. He supposed those men from the South who had been here at Johnson's Island would have given anything to see row upon row of white cotton in the hot sun shining down on the fields. But some had not returned.

To relieve the monotony Joe and the other workmen would often sing, and sometimes, mysteriously, they would all strike up the same tune. Not knowing how that happened, they would look at each other, puzzled, and shrug. Usually the songs were from "the other side." Joe and most of his fellow quarrymen were first-generation Italians. They had grown up cutting stone or trudging behind a load of cement from the time their young, tanned, well-muscled bodies could push a wheelbarrow.

The job superintendent who sat over in the remains of the old blockhouse intermittently reading his newspaper and dozing knew little about the history of the camp, and he seldom checked on the men in the quarry after mid-afternoon. If he had, he might have wondered more about the place. The quarry workers were not the only men who had sung on this island. The Confederate prisoners had done so, too. In order to keep their spirits up, night after night a chorus of voices would harmonize the notes of "Dixie," "Lorena," "The Bonnie Blue Flag," and other Southern songs.

These men were not to be entirely forgotten. Near the turn of the century there were efforts to commemorate the lives of those who had died there. The statue, called *The Outlook,* was executed in bronze by Moses Ezekiel, a soldier under General Lee who became a noted sculptor. It had been placed here by the Daughters of the Confederacy just after the turn of the century. The base was contributed by Mississippi; South Carolina gave the foundation of marble. On the northeast tip of the island is an acre of trees shading a graveyard. Here rest the remains of more than two hundred Confederate prisoners of war who died on Johnson's Island. Rotted wooden markers have been replaced, and at each grave now stands a headstone of Georgia marble on which is carved the name of the man and his regiment—a more

It Always Comes at Dark . . .

dignified commemoration, but whether wood or marble little comfort for a life lost.

"Santa Lucia," the quarrymen's voices rang out melodiously one afternoon at dusk, "Santa Lucia. . . ." When they concluded they went on to another tune. Joe Santos noticed that it began with a strange sort of humming. The men didn't seem to know the words, but they hummed the song as if they were going to start singing it any moment. He felt his lips begin to vibrate with the melody as they had when he was a child humming through a comb, and soon he could feel the vibration throughout his body. There was something plaintive about part of the tune; then the men's voices began to take on a lively, rousing quality filled with excitement. But no words came.

They cast surprised looks at each other. Never had they hummed together like this before. In a sense it was as if the song possessed them, and they were swept along by it, and the air all around them was filled with voices carrying the unfamiliar tune. Suddenly, with one accord, they stopped, and, somewhat abashed, they didn't look at each other. They were strangely silent until suddenly someone struck up another song, an animated version of the "Habanera." As if by agreement, no one mentioned what had happened.

Joe Santos noticed that as the summer passed and fall arrived, the humming occurred more often—always the same tune. It seemed to happen toward evening. The men began to grow increasingly nervous in the late afternoon, and several went to the superintendent with vague complaints and excuses, claiming that they soon would leave the island for other long-term employment that was open to them.

Finally, the superintendent was able to persuade someone to admit what was wrong.

"It's the song."

"What song?"

"The song we hear late in the afternoon when the sun begins to go down."

"Sing it!" bellowed the superintendent. But no one would.

"So you're quitting the job because of a song you don't know? You dumb wops. It's probably some opera nobody remembers."

Joe Santos flushed angrily. "It's no opera. I can't sing the words, but I can hum it for you."

"Well, whatcha know, Joe!" he said derisively. "Let's hear it then."

Santos began, and gesturing to the others, he waved at them to join in. The workmen hummed "Dixie" for the astonished superintendent without a wrong note.

"And others are singin' it with us. Lots of 'em," spoke up one of the group.

"So you think this island's haunted and that's the reason you want to quit. Right?" the superintendent said.

"This island no good," spoke up a worker.

"Ask him—the old white-headed man," said Joe Santos. And all eyes turned toward Giuseppe, who gazed over at the cemetery. He shrugged and spread his arms elegantly. "This song. She always come when the sun begin to touch the water." It was getting late then. "I no like'a here!" he said vehemently, and lifting his tools to his back, he strode toward the water. The dark heads of

It Always Comes at Dark . . .

the younger men nodded agreement, and they began to stop work, too. Everyone knew by now that the ground beneath their picks held the bones of the men in gray who had once sung this melody. Perhaps not all were resting peacefully in the cemetery.

But how did the mysterious rhythm find its way to the ears of people who were newcomers, strangers, foreigners? For days they had wondered at the unfamiliar melody, a tune so strong that with no conscious decision on the part of the men they began humming it. It was an uncomfortable sensation.

Giuseppe stopped and pointed a gnarled tan finger up at the statue of the Confederate soldier who stood with arm raised. "I think he hear it, too." The old man's lips were compressed as he gazed at the statue, and his head bobbed affirmingly.

While they were talking, the blue mist of evening began creeping in from the waters of Lake Erie, and the small white ferry approached. The men heard the lonely sound of its whistle and lost no time scurrying in the direction of the pier.

After that day they did not come back.

Sometimes, years later at dusk, when he was on another job, Joe Santos thought of the island. He remembered how nightfall brought out scores of shadowy gray figures gliding, gesticulating, gathering among the oak trees, and he knew that they were probably still singing. He had heard them sometimes even above the fierce roar of the winds off the lake. Singing always with that wild, plaintive quality a rousing song the superintendent had called "Dixie"—a song that to the prisoners meant home.

Andersonville—
Andersonville Prison consisted of huts surrounded by a stockade. A lack of food and medical supplies later in the war, due to the destruction of crops and blockade of Southern ports, caused a tragic loss of lives from malnutrition and disease. Overcrowding was prevalent, as it was at many prisons. Captain Henry Wirz, the commanding officer, was an incompetent and was later tried and executed.

The reconstruction of the prison may be visited today. It is nine miles northeast of Americus, Georgia.

○○○

ANDERSONVILLE'S GHOST RAIDERS

Andersonville, Georgia

"Rather be doin' this than anything I know," one prisoner said to the other.

"Yes," his companion replied grimly.

Scruffy, half-starved, and barefoot, one with a hammer and the other with a saw, they labored without rest in the heat of the day. They found the thump of hammer on nail, the pull of the saw deeply satisfying. By early afternoon their project began to take shape, and in the gray light of dusk, you could see its harsh black silhouette against the sky.

It was a sturdy gallows that the prisoners themselves had built at the order of the prison commander—their part in seeing that justice would finally be done.

A pall of hatred hung over Andersonville, the camp most dreaded by Federal prisoners, on that afternoon of July 11, 1864. Yet there was a kind of fierce joy, a savoring of vengeance, too, for tomorrow was hanging day, and the men to be hanged were the Raiders. They were just six of a gang of at least five hundred human vultures who had brutally preyed upon the entire camp.

The next day, while former companions watched and shouted curses, Confederate guards led the surly-faced men out of the small enclosure where they had been chained awaiting their fate. Each Raider was escorted up the gallows steps accompanied by the camp chaplain, Father Peter Whelan. There was Charles Curtis, Munn, Delaney, John Sarsfield, William Rickson. Several were Catholics and made a last confession. Father Whelan offered the crucifix to Rickson, but, an unbeliever, he jerked his head aside in annoyance. Last of all the leader, and the most feared of all the men, appeared—Willie Collins. The shouted insults of the crowd rose to a crescendo. He had no statement of penitence—not Willie. In fact, he had not even given his real name.

Captain Wirz, the camp commandant, watched, and somehow, without understanding it, he had a queasy feeling in his guts, a sense of foreboding. Why, he did not know, for he had seen many men hang.

"Hang them, hang them, hang them," chanted thousands of Yankee voices. "Hang them!"

Many Federal prisoners had suffered or had buddies who had been robbed, beaten, or murdered by this riffraff of the Union army. Collins and his men were even more contemptible than bummers—the deserters and marauding scum of both armies.

Meal sacks were drawn over the heads of the men standing on the gallows, and still the chorus of angry voices went on, fading only when all the kicking, choking hooded figures became limp, ragged scarecrows dangling from the rough gallows beam. Only then did the shouts die away.

Decades passed. The double stockade of pine logs sagged and fell. Maggots, flies, and vermin, robbed of the infected bodies of their human hosts, gradually sought their food elsewhere. Nature began to heal this infested area, renewing it with clean, fragrant things—pine, bay, sweet-gum, wild blackberries, and scrub oak. The small patch of wilderness was later reclaimed in a burst of enthusiasm for the history of the War Between the States, and the prison site fifty miles south of Macon where fourteen thousand Union soldiers died became Andersonville National Historic Site—Prison Park and National Cemetery.

Andersonville commander Captain Henry Wirz had not been a Southerner. He was a native Bavarian who used Georgia militiamen for prison guards. The militiamen were the dregs of the men left at home, for the best soldiers were in the regular army trying to stop Sherman.

One Saturday in July, 1990, Currie McClellan and Bill Blue headed down Highway 75 out of Atlanta and took the Highway 49 exit leading to Andersonville, nine miles northeast of Americus. Bill was a native Southerner. Currie, a Vietnam veteran and displaced Northerner, upon moving to Atlanta had developed an intense interest in the Civil War. Trips like this one had formed strong bonds of friendship between the two men, despite their differing sympathies.

Andersonville's Ghost Raiders

"I've heard that the ghost of Captain Wirz has been seen walking along this road," said Bill as Currie sped toward the Andersonville Historic Site in his silver Dodge Caravan. Currie didn't reply.

"Did you hear me?"

"I'm not into superstition, Bill. I'm here to learn as many facts as I can about what this place was like a hundred and twenty-five years ago. How it was for the men who lived here."

"Yeah. I know what you mean. I wasn't serious."

They stopped in Andersonville to get a Coke at a filling station, then passed the railroad depot where incoming northern prisoners de-trained from the Southwestern Railroad (now Central of Georgia) to march the quarter mile to the Prison Park.

"Well, we're here!" exclaimed Currie. He found himself giving a slight shiver. "Hard to realize thousands of Union prisoners died at this place."

"About thirteen thousand I think."

"My great-great-grandfather Currie was here. His stories came down in the family. Prisoners got something like a half pint of broth with a few cow peas in it, a little meat and moldy cornbread."

Bill was irritated. "What do you think the Confederate soldiers were eating? Fried chicken, salad greens, and biscuits? I think these fellows were lucky if they still had their boots and blankets when they got here. They were captured by Confederates who had nothing themselves."

"We're going to have to decide on a campsite soon. You realize the sun's about to set? Let's decide where to camp," Bill suggested.

Andersonville, Georgia

"Why not go into the village, get something to eat, and then come back and park just outside the gates? Think they'd let us do that?"

"Far as I know."

Two hours later they had eaten country ham and fried chicken at the historic old Windsor Hotel, stopped at a store to buy some milk and cereal for breakfast, and returned. They parked about a hundred feet from the cemetery gate.

Bill began to study a map of the prison camp. With his finger Currie tapped the sketch of the prison enclosure. "Sure looks small, doesn't it?" Both men knew that as many as thirty-five thousand people had been jammed into this area—enough for a small city—and it was only twenty-seven acres. A filthy stream, more like an open sewer, ran through the prison camp.

"They dropped like flies from disease. No wonder it was called a hell-hole." Bill, frowning, shook his head and stared over the land. They discussed how many good men were here, but others were vicious, living off killing and robbing their comrades.

"But the way they were treated is hard to excuse, Bill. Toward the last as many as a hundred and fifty men were dropping dead every day from scurvy and dropsy," said Currie, who was big on statistics. "Infected wounds, rotting limbs covered with maggots—smell was horrible. No doctors or medicine."

Bill had his own facts. "Doctors came out here, Currie, but they had no medicine to give the prisoners. When the Union blockade didn't let anesthetics or medical supplies get through the ports, prisoners suffered agonies just like the wounded Confederates. How do you share what you don't have yourself?"

Andersonville's Ghost Raiders

"There was food and medicine up north. If we could have exchanged Rebels in the prisons up there for the Union soldiers here, it would have saved thousands of our men."

"Sure. The Confederates in the prisons up north were praying for the same thing. Do you know why the exchange stopped?"

"No."

"Grant gave express orders."

"He did!" Currie was momentarily outraged.

"Sure. He thought the Rebels would be back fighting again, but he wasn't so sure of the Yankees."

Currie, whose ancestors came from New England, said, "Our men would have gone back and fought, too."

"Maybe. But fighting is more important when you're trying to protect your home."

Currie nodded. "That's true. But why not feed our men? This was a farm area, and lots of the prisoners died from scurvy and dropsy."

Bill couldn't believe how flimsy Currie's history was. "Currie! Most people didn't have full barns and farm animals left," he said. "The countryside had been plundered, crops burned by some of the very men whose names you see on these Union cemetery markers." Bill rubbed it in. "The Yankee commanders didn't worry about leaving enough to feed people."

"Don't get so touchy," said Currie.

"Let's walk over there." Bill was heading toward six graves over to one side. "These have got to be the graves of the Raiders."

"Who?"

"Some of your good Union boys, Currie. But not really. I guess you'd say they were more like the 'bummers' both armies were plagued with. The men buried here were the leaders of a gang of about five hundred such fellows who beat and murdered other men for extra food and whatever else they could steal."

"How did they get on to them?" asked Currie.

"One of the prisoners finally had the courage to complain to a guard, and the guard reported it to Captain Wirz."

"Wirz was no good."

"You're probably right. But surprisingly enough, he had some sense of fairness, and he ordered a detail of prisoners and guards to round up the ring leaders."

"The prisoners conducted the trial, didn't they?"

"Yes. Six particularly vicious characters received death sentences, and the prisoners themselves built the gallows inside the stockade. Captain Wirz had decided that they would also be the ones to execute the six Raiders. In the meantime a prisoner group who called themselves the Regulators formed their own police force in order to prevent other human debris from taking over after these men were executed.

Reading the Raiders' grave markers, Currie said, "Here's the ring leader of them all."

"Willie Collins?"

"Right. He dubbed himself Colonel Mosby after the Confederate guerrilla raider."

"An insult to Mosby if there ever was one. A fine man. Ever read the book *Mosby's Men?*"

Currie seemed not to have heard. "I despise guys like these Raiders—murdering and stealing from fellow prisoners already in the worst sort of misery. Damn their souls!" Currie spat on Collins's grave. "Hell's fire is too good for them."

Bill was shocked at his outburst but said only, "They sure didn't deserve to rest in peace, did they?"

They spread their air mattresses on the floor of the van.

"Think we'll be OK here or should we have parked at the RV campgrounds?" asked Currie.

"We'll be fine. Being away from the other tourists gives us more opportunity to absorb the atmosphere," said Bill. "Of course, it's hard to know it the way it was then. It's pleasant out here now."

Currie felt a vague sense of uneasiness but fell into a sound sleep almost immediately.

"I don't know why. It may be thinking about all the men who died here. Seems a little eerie out here to me." Bill had propped two pillows under his head and taken out a tiny battery-operated reading lamp. "Bother you if I read for awhile?" He looked over at Currie and saw that he was already sound asleep. In a short time he closed his book.

A breeze sprang up and tree leaves rustled faintly outside the van.

Not long after midnight Currie awoke and discovered what may have been the reason for his earlier restlessness—an unusually pungent odor.

He looked over at the sleeping man beside him and was instantly ashamed of his thought. It couldn't be Bill! The two men had been together since they had left Atlanta, and he had not caught a whiff of anything except aftershave. Perhaps one of Bill's children had left a pair of old, over-ripe sneakers in the van or the remains of a hamburger under a seat. But the odor was worse than that! He took the light and began to search. Then, although he was ashamed of himself, he couldn't resist

Andersonville, Georgia

focusing the tiny map light on one of Bill's bare toes to see if he spotted a world-class case of athlete's foot, but he saw only pink, healthy skin.

To his distress the smell became more odious by the minute—so sickening that he began to feel like gagging. Good Lord! How could he stand this? It smelled like human excrement—and the filth of creatures who had gone unwashed for months.

Was the odor stronger outside? He quietly slid back the side door of the van, placed the corner of his pillow in the crack so the door wouldn't latch, and stepped out into the night air. Good God! Now the stench enveloped and almost overwhelmed him. He felt his stomach begin to heave, and it was all he could do not to retch violently.

He began wondering if he were suddenly becoming ill and this was a symptom of his sickness. He had heard that some diseases started with the afflicted smelling a strange odor. Perspiration born of fear broke out upon his forehead. In China he had been told that odors sometimes signified the presence of an evil spirit. Ridiculous!

There was something familiar about this experience, however. He managed to place it—Vietnam, where streams reeking of raw sewage ran through the center of some of the small villages. But this odor was much worse. More like the sickening conditions of a military hospital in the jungle heat—an odor of gangrene, running pustulant sores, and the scent of putrescent wounds with unchanged dressings. He was afraid he would throw up if he took another breath.

Shreds of mist curled upward from puddles of rainwater. He stumbled a few steps and thought he heard the hoarse rasp of men's voices. If there were other campers out here, he'd better call Bill, and the two of them could investigate together. He slid back the door of the van, and to his surprise he saw Bill standing there wide awake, an old tan raincoat thrown over his pajamas.

"This terrible odor waked me up. I started to ask if you had noticed it, too, and I was surprised to see you were not in the van," exclaimed Currie.

"I had to find out where it was coming from."

"Well?"

"God knows. It's all around us."

"I thought some of the things in Nam were bad," said Currie, "but this is worse." And suddenly he was in Vietnam and experiencing it all over again. He began to tremble.

"Listen. You hear a noise, Currie?" Currie tried to recover himself but could not respond without stuttering. "M-m-m-maybe."

Bill laughed a bit uneasily. "We shouldn't have camped near a graveyard!"

"That's crazy," said Currie indignantly.

"Do you hear that noise? What in hell is it? Like the murmur of a crowd in the distance and above it something else. I'm getting my shotgun." Bill reached for the canvas gun bag.

"It's got to be thunder," Currie maintained.

"Sounds to me like men calling. Do you know what they are saying?" Bill stiffened in recognition. "It's Wil–lee, Wil–lee. Remember? Willie Collins was the Raiders' chieftain. Listen." He cocked his head to one side. "Do you hear it now?"

"N-no. Well . . . I'm not sure. I think I do hear something."

Andersonville, Georgia

"'Had-to-rob-them.' He's saying it very low, very slowly. 'Couldn't-have-survived-otherwise.' Man, what an eerie voice!"

"I hear a sound, but I'm not sure of the words," Currie admitted reluctantly.

Bill's voice was almost a whisper. "It's becoming more continuous—like a chant, deep and harsh. Good God! They're saying 'Hang them . . . hang them . . . hang them.'" The hair on Currie's arms stood up and his flesh crawled, despite his skepticism.

Small twisting spirals of mist were rising all around them, giving an eerie effect to the landscape, and Currie shuddered. Then he realized it was mist after the rain, for the ground was warm.

"Hang them . . . hang them . . . hang them." Hoarse voices seemed to merge into one. The moon went behind a cloud, and the horrible sound went on.

The two waited, too stunned to move. They heard an angry murmur that slowly mounted to a crescendo. Currie's superior manner was gone. He was horribly shaken, and his heart thudded violently. Finally the sound began to fade, become fainter, and in seconds, it was gone altogether. Currie's heart slowed its violent pounding. It was a minute or so before either he or Bill spoke. Somehow they were not yet ready to talk about the sounds they had heard.

Bill rose from his crouched position. One palm had landed in a puddle of water. He smelled his hand. The stench struck his nostrils with the force of a blow. Reluctantly he bent down to sniff the puddle, and the odor of the water was even worse.

The prisoners themselves tried and hanged the vicious Raiders.

Andersonville, Georgia

Finally Currie spoke. "Have you noticed the scent in the air has grown fainter?"

"Yes. A good deal. It's almost gone. Is it possible that the ground still holds the foul odor of the men in that camp, and that with rain or other conditions it may return?" asked Bill.

"Well, it's certainly from natural conditions," said Currie still clinging steadfastly to his skepticism. "Could be a paper mill."

"Oh, sure. Lots of industry around here," Bill said sarcastically. "I don't think so, Currie. I understand there's a place in Poland where a Nazi death camp buried so many bodies that the odor has sometimes been unbearable. No one has even been able to farm the land."

"Well, that may have some scientific basis," Currie replied. He tried to dismiss the voices from his mind. An odor was the sort of thing a man could deal with rationally.

"You know, it's the anniversary of the date the Raiders were hanged—July 11th," Bill said. But when he thought about it, if spirits really did return to Andersonville, a place that had seen so much horror, wouldn't one day be as likely as another? He wondered, too, whether other visitors had experienced any strange phenomena here.

The next morning the park personnel seemed puzzled. They had no explanation nor did they know of any such reports in the month of July in previous years. On the other hand, tourists did not usually lodge that close to the stockade itself.

Currie mused. "Odd. Captain Wirz himself would be hanging from the end of a rope only a year later at the

Old Capitol prison in Washington, D.C., convicted of brutality here. I guess such a possibility never occurred to him as he watched the Raiders getting theirs."

"Some of the kids think the ghost of Wirz still walks the road out there. Comes back because he feels guilty, I guess," the young park ranger commented jocularly to Currie. "But I'd say that's just imagination, wouldn't you?"

"I certainly don't believe in ghosts," Currie barked at him gruffly.

Bill shot Currie an ironic look. The ranger's face reddened. "Of course not. I understand that, sir," he said apologetically.

Fredericksburg—
One of the great battles of the Civil War took place from December 11 to December 13, 1862, and involved one hundred twenty thousand Union soldiers under General Ambrose E. Burnside, the new commander of the Army of the Potomac. His strategy, to sweep through Fredericksburg and on to Richmond, had merit but was undermined by inefficient bureaucracy, insufficient speed, and bad roads. Union troops attacking across unprotected fields toward the stone wall of the Confederate strongpoint, Marye's Heights, were easily repulsed by General Robert E. Lee. Lee, commanding seventy-eight thousand men, crafted an artillery defense that swept advancing Union troops with chilling efficiency, causing a loss of nine thousand Federals. Confederate losses were slightly over fifteen hundred.

Fredericksburg Battlefield, a unit of Fredericksburg and Spotsylvania Military Park, is near Interstate 95 at Fredericksburg, Virginia, forty-five miles south of Washington, D.C.

ooo

THE ANGEL OF MARYE'S HEIGHTS

Fredericksburg, Virginia

Acts of amazing courage in combat often go unrecognized and unrewarded, but during the Union campaign to take Fredericksburg there was an ordinary soldier whose bravery became legendary.

When it was obvious to Southerners in January, 1861, that guns would be used to settle what politicians either could or would not decide, a young South Carolinian named Richard Kirkland didn't wait to be called up. He joined the Camden Volunteers. In the spring of 1861, the Volunteers received orders to report to Charleston. They

The Angel of Marye's Heights

arrived at Morris Island just in time to see the opening shot of the war fired on Fort Sumter.

After the fall of the fort Kirkland's company of volunteers journeyed to Richmond and were mustered into the Confederate army in May, 1861. Kirkland was lucky enough to serve in the regiment of family friend Colonel J. B. Kershaw.

Richard Kirkland was restless. For him action couldn't come too soon. He fought, and he continued to fight—at First Bull Run, in the Peninsular Campaign, the Seven Days' campaign and the related battles of Seven Pines between General Robert E. Lee and Major General George B. McClellan. This last, which took place near Richmond, was a bloody Southern defeat, and both sides learned that victory could be purchased at the cost of too much bloodshed. Although wounded, young Kirkland was not a quitter. In April, 1862, at the end of his one-year enlistment, he re-enlisted in Company G, 2nd South Carolina, and was promoted to orderly sergeant. The men in the company were friends from his hometown of Flat Rock.

Camped two miles south of Fredericksburg, Virginia, in December, 1862, Kirkland and his company formed part of the brigade of Colonel Kershaw, who had been promoted to brigadier general after the battle of Bull Run. Kershaw's brigade was directly in the path of the Union army gathering just across the Rappahannock River under General Ambrose E. Burnside. The Union general planned to attack Richmond by way of Fredericksburg. He had hoped he could do this before Lee gathered his defensive forces, but repeated delays frustrated his plans. Now Lee's army lay in wait for him.

Fredericksburg, Virginia

In the early morning hours of December 11 Union engineers worked swiftly in the waters of the icy Rappahannock to lay a pontoon bridge. Fog over the river valley concealed their project. All went well until the rays of the sun burned through and Major General William Barksdale's Mississippians saw them. Concealed in cellars along the Fredericksburg waterfront, Confederates swept the bridge builders with gunfire. The laying of the bridge became more difficult.

Unfortunately, of the general's three "Grand Divisions" only two were able to cross. One headquartered in Fredericksburg; the other, under General William B. Franklin, took up position about a mile below town. Already two days behind schedule, Burnside was about to launch his two-pronged attack. But his delays had bought the time Lee needed. He was massed behind Fredericksburg to test his defenses.

General Franklin had sixty thousand troops at his disposal. On the morning of the 13th Burnside ordered him to use only forty-five hundred to attack Jackson, whose position was on open, flat land. Spotting a gap in General "Stonewall" Jackson's line, Franklin's men believed they were in luck. They surged toward it, until suddenly, bewilderingly, Union soldiers began to tumble like falling dominoes. Jackson's vicious artillery counterattack plugged the opening, driving them back. Franklin's tremendous reserves might have saved the day, but he did not have the daring to bring them up.

Above Fredericksburg is a ridge called Marye's Heights. The ridge was occupied by General James Longstreet, who had been joined by Stonewall Jackson. Arriv-

The Angel of Marye's Heights

ing from Winchester, Jackson had posted his corps on Longstreet's right. During the Federal delays, Lee was able to muster some eighty thousand men to meet the Yankees.

Burnside's objective was Marye's Heights, and blue-clad lines of men began charging up the slope toward a stone wall at the foot of the ridge. Thousands of rifle volleys met them, cutting the Union soldiers to pieces, but a few got to within forty yards of the wall. Even the gain of that distance worried Confederate general James Longstreet.

Just after midday he sent an order to General Kershaw, whose brigade was standing by on Telegraph Road: "Send two regiments to support hard-pressed Georgians and North Carolinians."

Kershaw sent the 8th, led by Colonel John D. Kennedy, and Sergeant Richard Kirkland's 2nd South Carolina. He himself had enrolled Kirkland in the Camden Volunteers two years before. Moving along Telegraph Road to Marye's Heights, exposed to a punishing fire, the two regiments reached the sunken road but not before losing twenty-eight men. Marching double-time they reached Cobb's Brigade.

As his regiment moved into battle, Kirkland turned to see General Cobb fall mortally wounded. Within minutes General Kershaw was given command, to replace the dying Cobb. Burnside continued to attack the Confederates throughout the afternoon, recklessly sending forward the divisions of Howard, Sturgis, Getty, and Humphreys to cross four hundred yards of open field under fire. If they survived the massed artillery fire, from behind the

Fredericksburg, Virginia

wall not two hundred yards away, a sheet of flame engulfed them from infantry. Union soldiers screamed and crouched as they tried to breast it.

Kirkland was among a section of riflemen six ranks deep. They fired consecutively from the sunken road in back of the wall. Burnside continued to order brigades—fifteen in all—to challenge the position. Finally the few Union soldiers lucky enough to still be alive staggered back under the sheltering slopes. They left sixty-three hundred dead and wounded comrades behind them. Near the stone wall lay the bodies of at least twenty-five brave men who had almost reached the Confederate line.

Behind the wall on Marye's Heights, Kirkland and his regiment dropped to the ground. They slept, exhausted, the main battle over. Next morning as a wintry, grayish pink tinged the horizon, the two armies still faced each other warily. The show of a head on either side brought a flurry of shots. The wounded Union soldiers were making a terrible din, groaning and crying out for assistance where they lay. The ground is cold in Fredericksburg in December.

Everyone was affected by the scene, and when Kirkland could stand their pleas no longer he sought out his regimental commander, Colonel John D. Kennedy, and asked permission to do something to comfort the wounded. Kennedy immediately refused, fearing the enemy would shoot Kirkland. Cries of agonizing pain and misery continued throughout the day.

That afternoon Kirkland was able to obtain permission to speak to General Kershaw. Brigadier General Joseph B. Kershaw, sitting upstairs viewing the battlefield from a window in the Widow Stevens's house, was sur-

Wounded Union soldiers were crying out for
assistance where they lay.

prised to see his fellow South Carolinian. Kirkland pleaded with the general to allow him to help the wounded Union soldiers, but Kershaw said it was "too dangerous."

"You will probably get a bullet in the head the minute you cross that wall, Richard," he answered. Kirkland, taking advantage of their personal friendship, continued his efforts to persuade him until Kershaw finally gave his permission.

"May I show a white handkerchief when I'm ready to go over the wall, sir?"

Reluctantly, Kershaw shook his head. "I'm sorry but they will take it as a signal of a general truce," said the General. "I hate to deny you that edge of safety, but they will misconstrue it."

Sergeant Kirkland was determined to go anyway, and he began by gathering as many canteens as he could carry. While his friends crouched behind the wall watching tensely, the young Confederate leaped over it and ran to the nearest wounded Union soldier. Union troops, eyeing his every move, must have known what he was doing. No one fired. Kirkland lifted the first man's head, gave him water, and covered him with an overcoat. Then he went on to the next. After exhausting all the water in the canteens the South Carolinian returned to the Widow Stevens's well and filled them again. His trips, in front of enemy guns, continued for more than an hour and a half as he went on giving water to all the wounded he could locate on that part of the battlefield before returning to his company.

Although there is no count of how many men he was able to help, he reached possibly a hundred—a relatively

The Angel of Marye's Heights

small number of those who covered the entire battlefield. But those men never forgot him. His act of mercy made Richard Kirkland a legend.

Kirkland's name would undoubtedly have been added to the Confederate Roll of Honor, the Southern equivalent of receiving the Medal of Honor, but the roll was not established until later. His reward was two months' leave for recruiting service in his home county—a parallel to present-day meritorious leave.

Rejoining his company during May, 1863, he was in the thick of the fighting at Chancellorsville and Salem Church. The next news of Kirkland is for an heroic act that occurred in July during the second day of the Battle of Gettysburg. Fighting his way with Kershaw's brigade through the peach orchard in an effort to smash the strong Union line along Plum Run, he was rewarded with a promotion to lieutenant. He would never officially receive it.

After Gettysburg Kirkland went by rail to Chickamauga to reinforce General Braxton Bragg in Tennessee. On the afternoon of September 20 Union general George H. Thomas held Snodgrass Hill, and his defense was so strong that he was known afterward as the "Rock of Chickamauga." Kirkland and his comrades repeatedly assaulted the hill. They went forward; they retreated; they hurled themselves at the Union lines again.

On one of these assaults Kirkland and two companions continued to advance. Suddenly, realizing that they were alone, they turned hurriedly to follow their company's retreat. Pausing, Kirkland wheeled to fire one more shot. As he did he was struck down by a single bullet in the chest.

Fredericksburg, Virginia

His last words were, "Save yourselves and tell my father I died right."

One soldier described the scene when Kirkland's body was brought home. "You couldn't hitch a horse within a quarter mile of his house there was such a crowd." Others said that the Kirkland house, which still stands, was spared by Sherman, "because even in 1865 Richard Kirkland's name had become a legend on the lips of soldiers in both North and South."

Under the large trees in Camden's quiet Quaker cemetery a large headstone marks his grave reading: "Richard Kirkland, C.S.A. At Fredericksburg he risked his life to carry water to wounded and dying enemies and at the Battle of Chickamauga laid down that life for his country. 1843–1863.

Richard Kirkland was not only a brave man but a compassionate one as well.

Antietam (also called Sharpsburg)—

On September 17, 1862, the battle of Antietam began at dawn with Major General Joseph Hooker's corps moving south along the Hagerstown Turnpike to assault Lee's left flank. Major General George B. McClellan massed his seventy-five thousand troops along the eastern bank of Antietam Creek against General Robert E. Lee on the west bank with scarcely thirty-eight thousand men. Fighting raged in the cornfield until General J. B. Hood counterattacked. Major General Edwin V. Sumner of the Union forces was caught in a Confederate cross fire and routed, and the battle shifted southward. Burnside struggled to cross Antietam Creek via the bridge and finally began to advance. Confederate General A. P. Hill arrived from Harpers Ferry just in time to drive back the Northerners, rescue Lee's army, and end the battle.

Antietam National Battlefield is near State Route 65 at Sharpsburg, Maryland, twelve miles south of Hagerstown.

OOO

"YANKEES" SAVE LEE'S ARMY

Antietam, Maryland

Blood from a head wound trickled from his forehead down the young Union officer's cheek. He lay there and moaned, half conscious, while through the pain his bewildering recollections were of a nightmare—a horrifying dream. Lieutenant Charles Schwarz of the 51st New Yorkers was to learn that September 17, 1862, was a day when events were not always what they seemed and misconceptions could turn a stalemate into a victory.

Here at Antietam the Union's golden opportunity came to end the war quickly. Lee's battle lines were frayed and sparse, and Confederate forces waved their

Antietam, Maryland

regiment flags vigorously to create the illusion of strength. Bluffing in order to hold parts of their line, the Confederates actually had no reserves and were demoralized.

Along the road called Bloody Lane, two armies fought until nearly five thousand men in blue and gray lay dead. The Union lost General Rodman, and white-haired old General Sumner, shaken by the killing he had seen that day, assumed that half the Federal army was scattered. He sent a gloomy message to General McClellan, saying that if he continued the attack he could expect a Confederate counterattack and find himself without reserves. McClellan—saddened by the death of so many men, underestimating the still-undamaged spirit of his battlewise regiments, and, as usual, overestimating the numbers of Confederates—upheld General Sumner's decision. Ten thousand fresh Federal troops under General Franklin stayed where they were. Little did the Union commanders know that these ten thousand could have defeated Lee's entire army. Because of this decision the Confederates survived to fight for almost three more years.

The Battle of Antietam started in a misty, rainy dawn near the small whitewashed Dunker Church. In the late morning Union troops were trying to cross Antietam Creek, which was like a moat protecting a castle with the Confederates as the defenders. Low hills and sloping meadows bordered the east side of the stream. Here was the Army of the Potomac's 9th Corps, and General McClellan planned for the Federal troops to attack the Confederates on the high ground of the western bank opposite them.

"Yankees" Save Lee's Army

The two armies lay close together, between them the valley of Antietam Creek and the creek itself—about fifty feet wide but so shallow a man could walk across it in water below his waist.

For some reason Union troops behaved as if they were gazing at the mighty Mississippi, treating Antietam Creek as if it were impassable. No one thought of trying to swim the stream to test the depth of the water as young Custis Lee had once tested the Chickahominy for Stuart. On the east side a meandering country road led to the one narrow bridge across the creek, through a winding ravine and up to Confederate-held high ground. After twenty-four hours of examining the terrain—there was said to be a ford half a mile or so down the road, but no real effort was made to find it—the narrow bridge was still the Union command's only idea of the way to cross the creek and attack the Rebels. But just beyond the bridge they faced a sheet of fire from Confederate guns.

Waiting a couple of hundred yards back from the bridge in a protected valley were Colonel Edward Ferrero's two favorite regiments, the 51st New York and the 51st Pennsylvania. He challenged them to attack.

"Take that bridge at General Burnside's special request," Ferrero exhorted. He was standing only a short distance away from Lieutenant Schwarz.

"Colonel, will you give us our ration of whiskey if we make it?" shouted a Pennsylvania corporal. There was no rationing on either side in the Civil War, but whiskey was sometimes issued after a battle or used as a reward. Schwarz smiled and waited for the colonel's response.

"Yes, by God!" replied Ferrero passionately, and his men cheered. They dashed full tilt for the bridge, shout-

Antietam, Maryland

ing, falling in a wild melee of screams and yells, every second being mown down like grass by Confederate cannon and sharpshooters, with the Rebel ranks only twenty-five yards away. Schwarz and his comrades had never experienced anything like this. Another New Yorker later described the struggle saying, "The fire and smoke, flashing of muskets and whizzing of bullets, yells of men . . . were perfectly horrible."

Some of them were getting over the bridge, but there were more who needed to reach the other side who had not yet joined them.

General Rodman, a quiet, conscientious man who had been sent downstream to find a ford, had chosen a local farmer as a guide and spent the entire morning following him first to this place and then to that. Finally he began to suspect the farmer was a Southern sympathizer. Meanwhile the 8th Connecticut, off scouting the stream on their own, found a place so shallow everyone could wade it, and after this momentous discovery, Rodman prepared to attack Lee's right. But it was not long until things began to go wrong again.

Schwarz continued to lead his men across ravines and gullies, some of the worst terrain they had encountered. The upper slopes, planted with corn, formed an ideal cover for the Confederates, and in the field waited the Rebels, plentiful as the ears of corn and just as quiet. When the blue coats were close enough they laid down a devastating fire. At the same time a Confederate battery on Rodman's flank plowed him with rifle fire, and sharpshooters from behind a stone wall at the top of the hill picked off his men by the score. Antietam was to become the worst one-day bloodbath of the Civil War.

"Yankees" Save Lee's Army

As Schwarz and his troops straggled up a hill under intense fire, their commander ordered them to lie down. When they obeyed, chunks of earth flew up all around them, and a searing barrage of shot and shells swept over the unfortunate men. This was far worse than charging, Schwarz thought—this helpless lying on their stomachs to be shelled. His own men and those along the entire Federal line burst into shouts of the most horrible swearing. He could take it no longer, and as his men saw him rise, they too were scrambling to their feet, running desperately straight toward the cornfield and the Confederates. Losses were devastating. I'll die here, Schwarz thought, but so far a bullet had only grazed the side of his head. He continued to race toward the cornfield.

Union forces tried to regroup, but as General Rodman brought up the 4th Rhode Island to reinforce the Connecticut boys, he and his men stopped in amazement. Row upon row of blue coats charged from the cornfield, firing as they came.

Schwarz looked at them in astonishment. Now his men not only had a blue line behind them but one in front firing upon them as well, and they were thoroughly confused. Men in blue were fleeing pursued by other men in blue, and in the midst of this up came the Ohioans. Naturally perplexed by the scene before them, the Ohioans held their fire. On came the charging blue-clad figures, and at the instant before Lieutenant Schwarz was hit, he realized they were not comrades.

According to the story the lieutenant was fortunate enough to be able to tell many years later, this is how a regiment of "Blue-coats" played their part in defeating McClellan's army at the Battle of Antietam. The men

Antietam, Maryland

emerging from the cornfield were Confederate soldiers. Many had made do with ragged uniforms or civilian clothing. Lacking factories in the South to take their raw cotton and wool and supply them with the gray uniforms of the Confederacy, they were only too glad to put on the fine, new Federal uniforms captured in a recent raid at Harpers Ferry.

That one event generated enough confusion among the Union soldiers on this sector of the battlefield to make the entire Federal line fall back.

Fort Davis—
A key post, Fort Davis played a major role in the history of the southwestern frontier. Today the remains are more extensive and impressive than those of any other southwestern fort.

Fort Davis National Historic Site is on the northern edge of the town of Fort Davis, Texas. The fort can be reached from Interstate 10 on the north or U.S. 90 on the south.

FORT DAVIS AND THE TELLTALE ROSES

Fort Davis, Texas

In 1854 General Persifor Smith selected the site of a new fort to protect settlers against the Indians near Limpia Creek, Texas. It was a box-canyon with a backdrop of rugged, scenic mountains named for Secretary of War Jefferson Davis, later president of the Confederacy. Fort Davis's position was highly vulnerable. Hostile Comanches and Apaches could approach it without being discovered.

Lieutenant Colonel Washington Seawell, thinking that the fort should later be moved to a more strategic place at the mouth of the canyon, carried out the orders he received but built only temporary pine-slab houses for the officers. He constructed six stone barracks across the mouth of the canyon for the enlisted men.

Troops at Fort Davis immediately began to guard wagon trains and stage coaches on the San Antonio–El Paso road and rescue travelers from the Indians. Fort Davis became a key post in the defense system of West

Fort Davis, Texas

Texas. Manned by brave and courageous men, the forts in this system were strung from the Dakotas to the Texas border, from Kansas to California. There were Fort Stockton and Fort Davis in Texas, Fort Union in New Mexico, Fort Bowie in Arizona, and Fort Laramie in Wyoming.

A coach, on its way along the route near Fort Davis, might find itself surrounded by a cloud of dust raised by the hoofs of galloping Apache ponies. The Apaches would fall upon the passengers. Some passengers were lucky enough to reach Fort Davis, others were murdered.

The Fort itself was crudely built, for the first plan was to build it quickly and replace the buildings at a later time. Made of pine slabs set upright in the ground, the structures had plank or packed earth floors, roofs of canvas or thatched grass, and glazed windows. There were thirteen houses for married soldiers and their families, a hospital, a stable, a store and a billiard room. Compensations for this rough life were the beautiful scenery and a large vegetable garden for the garrison.

As war clouds began to loom over the South, they also darkened over Southerners on the western frontiers. In Colorado the gold miners from Georgia who had founded Denver, some of them hoping to settle there permanently, began to experience a hostile attitude from families who were arriving from the North and Midwest.

At Fort Davis the officers were from both North and South, and many had gone to West Point together. In fact one third of these West Pointers would soon join the Confederacy. Relations at parties and social events for the officers and their wives grew strained. As the South came closer to secession, arguments between officers at

Fort Davis, Texas.

Fort Davis, Texas

Fort Davis who had been friends became more heated. The relationship of one of the Southern officers and Fort Davis commander, Captain Edward D. Blake, became one of cold silence broken only by whatever orders were necessary.

One of the loveliest young women at the fort was Alice Walpole, the wife of a lieutenant from Alabama. Often homesick, missing the more gentle blue-green hills and wide rivers of her home state, it was not surprising that after the long, harsh winters she was filled with longing for the balmy days and flowers of a Southern spring. It was April, and it occurred to her that somewhere on this desert-like land, or among the jagged cliffs and ominous mountains, even now roses might be in bloom.

Wrapping herself in her long bright blue wool cape, Alice left the house on officers' row, passed the post garden, and was soon outside the fort. She stooped for a moment and cupped her hand to drink from the clear, fresh waters of Limpia Creek and appreciate its sparkling beauty in the sunlight. Then she headed on toward the mountains. They had always made her feel insignificant as she approached them, as small as one of the calm-faced china dolls with pink cheeks and painted black hair that she had played with as a child. She would never feel at home here. This land did not have the green, rolling landscape of her native Alabama, and there was a harshness in its beauty.

Following Limpia Creek she recalled someone saying that in the wilderness beyond the fort, beautiful white roses bloomed. This was desert country. She picked her way among the boulders and then began to climb, think-

Fort Davis and the Telltale Roses

ing the flowers might be found at higher elevations. Sometimes Alice thought she detected the scent of roses. Their fragrance drew her on. Once she looked back and the fort was now a dot in the distance.

She thought of Apaches, but there were always reports of them, and she reasoned that they normally lurked close to the trail leading to and from Fort Davis. Stage coaches carrying money boxes and passengers were more often their prey. She continued to follow Limpia Creek until suddenly she rounded a bend in the stream. Only a few feet away Indian braves were drinking water from the stream, their horses tethered nearby.

When her husband returned that afternoon, Alice was not at home, nor was she anywhere about the fort. Before dark a party of soldiers went out and looked for her as long as there was light. A search party the following day, covering the surrounding area, checked with the families of Diedrick Dutchover and E. P. Webster, two stagecoach drivers who lived in the area. They could find no trace of her, and her husband was desperately worried.

Late one night a few months later a beautiful young woman was seen hurrying past the long row of officers' houses. Her cape billowed around her whipped by the west wind. A lieutenant saw her and, greeting her, he could hardly be sure she replied, for her voice seemed to be wafted away. What was it that appeared so familiar about her? He turned to look back and walked after her calling out, "Wait! Miss," but she vanished. He knew her. It was Alice Walpole!

From then on others began to report seeing the apparition of a beautiful woman, often near the quarters

Fort Davis, Texas

where the Southern wives gathered to do needlework and socialize. Perhaps she missed them, this girl who was so far from her native hills of Alabama. None ever heard her speak. The most tangible evidence of her presence was the sudden strong odor of roses in a room or a few wild white roses found mysteriously here or there.

After Jefferson Davis ordered the firing on Fort Sumter at Charleston, seven Southern officers called simultaneously at the commandant's office with letters of resignation before heading East to volunteer. Three of these former West Pointers would become brigadier generals in the Confederacy.

In the midst of the confusion the commandant noticed that on his desk was a vase of fragrant white roses, a strange phenomenon for this time of year. As one by one the Southern officers presented their letters of resignation, he said musingly to himself: "Seven white roses and seven resignations—what a coincidence!"

The fort was abandoned after the Confederates occupied it briefly in 1861, and it did not reopen until 1867. After the Civil War, when Southerners once more returned to Fort Davis, the ghost of the lovely girl is said to have returned with them. She was most often glimpsed in the quarters of lonely or homesick young wives.

And even today—whenever wild roses are found at an unexpected season of the year—the presence of Alice is suspected.

Fort Davis and the Telltale Roses

ooo

Fort Davis was occupied by the Southerners in 1861. They decided to march through New Mexico and toward Fort Union north to capture the gold fields, but they were turned back at Glorietta Pass in March, 1862, when their wagon trains were destroyed. They were forced to retreat east to join other Confederate troops.

Gaines Mill, Virginia—
The Seven Days' campaign beginning June 25, 1862, ended a three-month Union effort to capture Richmond. The armies of General Robert E. Lee and Major General George B. McClellan fought from the Chickahominy Swamps to the James River. Gaines Mill was the week's largest and most bloody engagement.

Gaines Mill battlefield, a unit of Richmond National Battlefield Park, is southwest of Richmond, Virginia, near State Route 156.

OOO

LATE HOMECOMING

Gaines Mill, Virginia

It is early morning in June, 1991, and sunlight rests softly on the unpainted two-story farm house at the edge of the clearing—the restored Watts House. Green fields stretch off in the distance, and the scene appears idyllically calm and peaceful. But if you stand and gaze at the yard and the fields for long enough and think about this place, its peacefulness may fade. The stillness may produce a sense of unease or perhaps raise the fine hairs on your arms. What is the old expression? A feeling that someone is walking over your grave.

You know that *something really does exist out there* in that terrible quiet. Whether it is the mysteriously reoccurring ring of a shot echoing in the air or shadows left imprinted in time drifting toward you across that expanse of shimmering green field, it is an impression that cannot, will not, go away.

Late Homecoming

After the firing on Fort Sumter President Lincoln's secretary of war wired the governor of North Carolina to raise troops to send down to discipline their rebellious sister state. "What? Go down and fight South Carolinians?" said Jim Jernigan's pro-Union father when he heard the news. "That's crazy. Would Washington ask Wisconsin for troops to discipline the people of Illinois?"

When word of the telegram reached the people of North Carolina there were no fence-sitters. Jim's father supported the youth's desire to enlist in the Confederate forces, and the tanned lanky farm boy left home for Camp Ellis at Raleigh, North Carolina. What a hurry he had been in to get here, and what an uncomfortable place it turned out to be, with its miserable log huts. He thought wryly of home and his parents. It would be hard on them without his skilled hands plucking the bolls in September and October when the time came to get the cotton from the fields before the fall rains. Like many other small North Carolina farmers, the Jernigans had no slaves and did the work themselves. But Jim knew the war wouldn't last long. He'd be back soon—not in time for this fall's crops—it was already June, 1862—but surely by next September.

After fighting and marching back and forth between the Chickahominy and the James, the Twentieth North Carolina was now encamped northeast of Richmond, Virginia, near Gaines Mill and Cold Harbor. Lieutenant Jernigan now considered himself a seasoned soldier. Everyone was tired but felt a sense of expectancy like that before an approaching thunderstorm. Without being told just when or where, the men knew there would be a

Gaines Mill, Virginia

big battle soon. General Lee had taken Joe Johnston's place, and although Lee had been in command for less than a month, the men said he was already giving McClellan a fit.

Except for Richmond, where Jernigan's friends had oohed and aahed, pointing at the beautiful buildings, the young North Carolinian wondered what there was to fight for out here in the middle of nowhere. He had never thought much about battle sites until lately.

"I thought the big battles were fought over a town or some important place," he said to a Virginian. "Why are we fighting out here in the midst of nowhere?"

"Lee wants to stop the Yankees before they get too close to the capital," his friend replied, "but the real objective is to kill more of them than they kill of us—to make this invasion of the South so damaging they'll quit. So it doesn't matter where we meet them."

It was mid-afternoon of June 26 when Jernigan, sent out to scout, stopped at a comfortable-looking unpainted two-story farmhouse. It reminded him of his parents' home. He would ask here for water for his horse and get any information he could. Tying the big bay near the back steps, he knocked and a woman in her seventies came to the door. She opened it a crack and saw a tall young man with brilliant blue eyes, a boyish face with a turned up nose, and light brown hair streaked with gold from the sun.

"Who be you?" she asked cautiously.

"Name of Jim Jernigan."

"Well, I'm Sarah Watts. What do ye want?"

"Just a soldier trying to get back to my regiment and

keep out of the way of the Yankees," he drawled in his soft North Carolina brogue.

"There be plenty of them around here, so you'd best look sharp."

"May I water my horse, ma'am, and fill my canteen?"

"You shore can if you'll draw me some water from the well, too."

When he had filled several buckets of water for her, the hospitable Mrs. Watts brought out some food from the safe over the big wood stove, and Jernigan ate hungrily. He didn't know when he'd last had homemade biscuits, crisp fatback, and black-eyed peas.

"Mighty tasty, ma'am."

She tried to smile, but her face was drawn and sad. Settling herself in a rocker near the fireplace, she watched him eat at the kitchen table. He sat in a pine chair with a thick slab of a seat and a Windsor back. He liked this house. On the table there were fragrant lavender roses from the yard in a glass jar, a pitcher of molasses, a round pat of butter with a raised wheat design. On the mantle were a china shepherd and shepherdess in shades of blue, rose, and gold and over them on the wall hung a cross-stitched Scripture verse. The kitchen was comfortable . . . homey, and he thought again of his parents.

Mrs. Watts was a widow and in poor health. No wonder she had been upset since Union general Porter's adjutant had visited to tell her the general would be taking over her house for his headquarters. Her granddaughter, a pretty girl of about eighteen with long brown hair, entered the kitchen.

"He and his men will be here at dawn to move us out,"

Gaines Mill, Virginia

said Mrs. Watts, staring at him hard, her hands twisting the handkerchief in her lap into a knot.

He didn't know how to comfort her, and he felt sorry for them. The girl gazed at him saying nothing, but he saw a flicker of hope in her eyes. "Will they give us the house back soon, Lieutenant Jernigan?" she asked.

"I imagine so, miss. 'Specially if we push them back a good distance," he replied reassuringly.

"It would be only right. Grandmother has always owned this house, Lieutenant."

Jernigan nodded sympathetically and looked into her eyes which had begun to sparkle a bit. Of course he had no idea what the Yankee general would do or what might happen to this house, but he couldn't tell the ladies that. So this was to be the Union headquarters. He wished that somehow he could spare them all this, what with the old lady sick and all.

"The Yankees are only a few miles from here, Lieutenant," Mrs. Watts said. "General Fitz-John Porter's camp has more men than I ever seen." Her voice was trembling. "I've heard tell there's more of 'em on the other side of the Chickahominy, too."

"There probably are," he said as he rose. "Well, ma'am, I shore do thank ye for the first good victuals I've had since I left home." Mrs. Watts's eyes brightened with pleasure. The girl seemed to be studying his face.

"I can show you the direction of the Yankee camp," she said. She walked out with him into the yard and pointed. "It's down an old logging road on the other side of that little stream. Would you want to see it?"

"Wal, don't believe I'll bother General Porter today,"

Late Homecoming

he drawled, smiling. "But I may be on his coattails tomorrow." He stared down at her for a moment.

"You shore are pretty. Reckon someday I could come back to see you?"

She blushed and nodded, then ran lightly up the steps and inside.

Jim considered what he had learned. The general must be planning to position his men in front of the house and probably put another line right behind the ravine. Of course, the swamp would be full of soldiers, too. This information and some of his speculating would be a piece in the puzzle that his commanding officers would use as they drew up their battle plans. He mounted his large bay and stared back at the Watts house. He would try to make an opportunity to see her granddaughter again. But for now—get going, Jernigan told himself, spurring his horse to a canter along the trail through the woods. It better be before the Yankees show up, or you might not stay alive to see that girl again. You may not anyway. Alive . . . stay alive—that was the refrain going through his mind as he rode, and he knew why. It was because of yesterday and Joe Godwin.

His friend was gone now. He still couldn't take it in. Godwin was one of the two men who had been with him since Camp Ellis at Raleigh. When he and Joe and Bill Corbitt made it through the first battles they'd become pretty confident. More confident as time went on. But now there were only two of them—riding together, talking in quiet voices by the camp fire at night. When would they feel like laughing and joking again?

Gaines Mill, Virginia

Why did one man live and another die? He shivered slightly. The loss of his friend brought death real close, and he hoped he would survive the battle that he knew was coming. Jim suddenly wanted very much to live. He wanted to see Mrs. Watts's pretty brown-haired grand-daughter after it was all over.

The morning of June 27, 1862, dawned hot and sultry. General Porter's men arrived, and, mopping their faces from the heat, they carried Sarah Watts out on her sickbed, loading a few of her belongings around her in the farm wagon. She wouldn't talk to the "Yankees." Taking a last look at her house, tears slid down her cheeks. She wiped them away quickly with the back of her hand. The Yankee soldiers had hung their shirts on her cape jessamine and forsythia bushes—she did hope they wouldn't trample them—and were already busy with their shovels throwing up a breastwork of logs and earth in front of the house.

In the brush of the swamp bottom perspiring soldiers under Union general George W. Morell were already trying to form a line and complaining about the tenacious vines and muck. Others took up a position above them along the crest of the ravine, then sat down and began to clean their guns, talk quietly, or try to bite through a piece of hardtack from their haversacks. There was nothing now but to wait—wait for the Rebels to come after them across that open ground. Artillerymen were dragging the big guns into position, ready to cut the enemy down the way a scythe slashes through wheat and lays it flat. Miserably hot, they swiped at mosquitoes, bit off pieces from plugs of tobacco, and chewed thoughtfully.

Late Homecoming

Somebody had a homemade cribbage game that he played silently with a fellow soldier.

About 2:30 P.M. General Morell heard the blood-curdling yell, and no matter how often he had heard it before, it always sent a chill down his spine. Rebs spilled out of the pine woods and began racing toward them across cultivated fields. Union artillery roared into action, transforming the fields into a fiery landscape of hell, but the men came on.

About five hundred of General Maxcy Gregg's South Carolinians made it through the artillery fire, plunged into the swamp, slogged across the creek and up the slope of the ravine. Ordered to stop and rest briefly, the South Carolinians sat on the ground at the edge of the ravine and spotted the flamboyant uniforms of a thousand New York Zouaves. They found them of more than passing interest with their bright red baggy pants, white canvas leggings, red sashes, short blue jackets, and tasseled red caps. What perfect targets they made.

"Let's get ourselves some Zouaves, boys," said one.

"Are they good to eat?" quipped another, and then the South Carolinians charged, killing about half the Zouaves before being forced to fall back. That afternoon Union artillery devastated other Confederates trying to advance across the fields, but Southern infantry lines behind them held firm against repeated Union assaults.

Lieutenant Jernigan of the Twentieth North Carolina charged General Sykes's men and, finding a piece of artillery within reach that was something the Twentieth could use, he coveted it. Elated, the Southerners pulled the needed gun back to their own lines. There was a brief lull in the firing, and Jernigan heard a colonel ask, "Has

The Twentieth North Carolina captured the Union gun.

Jackson gotten here?" Another officer replied, "Not yet." "Stonewall" Jackson and his men were on the way to reinforce them but their guide had taken a wrong road.

Many of the men around Jim collapsed from the heat. It was terribly hot, terribly humid, he thought, but no hotter than at home during the summer. The air reverberated with the sharp crack of gun fire. Unexpectedly the Sixteenth New York was countering with a fierce attack, forcing Lieutenant Jernigan and his company back. Loading and reloading, Jernigan fought on. Sometimes he couldn't see for the smoke. Shells whizzed past.

The Sixteenth New York seemed determined to retrieve the artillery the North Carolinians had taken with such desperate effort. The Yankees were shouting with glee and fighting hard when Jernigan plunged angrily into their midst to prevent Union soldiers from retaking the big gun.

He had picked off three and was aiming at the fourth when he felt a terrible thudding blow strike his chest. His hand clutched at the wound and came away wet from the spurt of warm blood through a gaping tear in his uniform. He didn't stop to think about it. The big gun—who was there to help secure it? He raised his revolver, aimed it toward a Union soldier who was straining over the weight of the piece of artillery, and got him. Then it seemed to the lieutenant that the cannon, and the men trying to help him, were spinning around and around and around. He moaned and fell beside the artillery piece. The last sight young Jernigan's uncommonly brilliant blue eyes ever saw was that big gun being dragged back toward the Union lines.

Gaines Mill, Virginia

The battle at the place called Gaines Mill—sometimes Cold Harbor—continued for four hours, and it was not until late afternoon that Jackson and his three divisions finally arrived. Lee now had his entire command, fifty-six thousand men, massed to attack. The Confederate columns formed, and by about 7:00 P.M. ninety thousand soldiers eyeballed each other across Boatswain's Swamp, Rebels and Yankees now only yards apart. The men in the ranks waited. It was up to the generals to decide what moves to make next and when. Union general Fitz-John Porter described "An ominous silence." The eerie quiet lasted for almost two hours.

On the Confederate side of the stand-off Lee rode his white horse Traveler up beside General John Bell Hood and gestured over at Porter's troops.

"Can you break his line?" He stared at the bold general searchingly. Both men were striving to make the right decision. Lee was ready for an all-out assault on Union defenses. As he scanned the blue-clad lines Hood's face was taut.

"I will try," Hood replied. He waved his hat in the air at the waiting soldiers behind him and galloped forward, his brigade of Texans and Colonel Evander Law's Georgians spearheading the attack. Surprised to see a gap in the Union line, Hood personally led their brigades into the opening. When they reached it they saw the grim reason the gap was there. The ground was covered with A. P. Hill's men, savaged earlier by Union general Porter's artillery fire. Confederates lay all over the grassy field—screaming, bleeding, dying amid smoke and bursts of gunfire. To prevent what they considered a suicidal act, men who were still alive reached up with desperate

Late Homecoming

hands and grasped at the legs of the Texans and Georgians running past them, as artillery fire ripped through the ranks. But their comrades, voicing the wild Rebel yell, raced on.

Down the wooded slope they dashed, splashed gratefully through the cool water of a shallow stream, and then they rushed General Richard Taylor's brigade with terrible fury. Nothing could stop them. Regiments fled before them in disorder. For the first time the Confederates pierced the enemy line, and the entire Union front was breaking into a retreat.

As a large crimson sun slid below the horizon, in the deep woods, among clumps of gathering darkness and across bullet-mown fields blanketed by dusk, a Union withdrawal began toward the Chickahominy River. Lee's exhausted soldiers dropped to the ground and slept where they were while others searched the battlefield for friends. The crops, underbrush, and trees that had daubed the fields with green that morning were gone, sheared off by artillery fire. Now the earth was stained blue and gray and red—a horror of shattered limbs, a field of bodies of both Confederate and Union soldiers torn apart and scattered as if by a monster. Here in the fields around the Watts House Lee had achieved his first major victory against McClellan.

Sarah Watts's yard was awash with a sticky moist red draining from wounded men and dead. So thick they lay around the house that nowhere was there to tread without stepping upon a body. What a blessing it was that she never saw it. Her granddaughter returned two months later to find the house a shell, riddled with bul-

Gaines Mill, Virginia

lets. Walls and roof were torn by shot and shell, weather-boarding honeycombed by mini-balls, every pane of glass shattered. On the floors—the immaculate floors her grandmother had taken such pride in—she saw scarcely a space of flooring as large as a man's hand that did not bear the dark purple stain of blood. Now a tenantless foul wreck, the once comfortable home was a harrowing spectacle that the girl recorded in her diary. Even in the corners of the yard were graves, and bordering the house was a long burial trench. Another trench in the garden was said to contain forty dead, and the fields around the house were filled with gruesome debris.

Jernigan, the North Carolina farm boy cut down by a Union bullet, would never feel sadness over the destruction of the Watts place nor anxiety as to whether he would see the girl again, nor concern over his parents' struggle to get in the fall crops. He would not worry about anything ever again, for he lay on last winter's smooth pine needles in the now quiet woods.

Two years later soldiers marching through Cold Harbor saw skeletons left from the battle, bony hands reaching up from the soft earth of the forest floor. There would be one last battle here, and it, too, would be a Southern victory. Lee would defeat Grant at this same place in June, 1864. This time more men would die on these fields, so that one would be able to walk across four acres of bodies and never have to place a foot upon the blood-soaked ground.

Sitting on the bank of Boatswain Creek in the 1980s, over a century later, a fisherman lay back and felt the earth give beneath his elbow. Down his arm sank until

Late Homecoming

it struck something hard and became caught in a viselike grip. When he managed to wrest his arm free he peered through the leaves into the hole and stared into the empty eye-sockets of a human skull. Horrified, the fisherman ran. But the next day he had recovered his courage and returned with a friend and a shovel. They dug up the skeletons of two hastily buried soldiers. Even now, in the 1990s, the remains of men are discovered in the peaceful green fields that surround the restored Watts house, as well as at other Virginia battle sites.

And what about these men who once longed to go home? What of their bones, their skulls bereft of the eyes that saw the horrors of that day, their mouths that cried out at the last, "Mother!" or "God, help me!" Many still lie here beneath the earth at Gaines Mill and perhaps their spirits abide here, too. Will they ever leave this place? From the intense, palpable quiet of the sunny summer day comes no answer.

It took one North Carolina soldier until 1991 to reach home. The buttons of his uniform, found with his skeleton, identified his native state, and the soldier was returned in the spring. He was given a funeral with full military honors, and hundreds were sufficiently moved to attend the rites and interment.

Who was that North Carolinian? Once he was more than just bones! He had a family and a name. Could it possibly have been Jim Jernigan?

Gettysburg—

The battle of Gettysburg, July 1 to July 3, 1863, was the great battle of the Civil War. In the last days of June, General Robert E. Lee, with seventy-five thousand soldiers, learned that ninety-five thousand men under Major General George G. Meade were within striking distance. There was fighting on July 1, but most of the remainder of both armies arrived that night and the next morning. At four in the afternoon Confederate general John B. Hood's division swept around the Union left flank and overran Devil's Den to begin the ascent of Little Round Top, which overlooked the entire Union position. After Confederate attacks and counterattacks at Culp's Hill, the second day ended. At daylight the Confederates renewed the attack, but the Union position was too strong. In the afternoon Longstreet's veterans and Pickett's fresh divisions—about fifteen thousand men—moved forward. A Union eyewitness described it as "an overwhelming resistless tide of an ocean of armed men sweeping upon us." Pickett's charge was the climax of the battle. Union reinforcements struck and the Confederates withdrew. Total casualties were about fifty thousand.

Gettysburg National Military Park is on U.S. Route 15 (business) at Gettysburg, Pennsylvania, thirty-seven miles southwest of Harrisburg.

○○○

A MYSTIC POWER AT GETTYSBURG

Gettysburg, Pennsylvania

This story is about a moment when the choice of one road over another was critical to the future of a nation, when the guidance seen by an entire regiment of men was so bizarre that it can only have come from the realm of the supernatural.

On July 1, 1863, the Twentieth Maine under Colonel Joshua Chamberlain and Colonel Adelbert Ames's brigade were heading north from Maryland into Pennsylvania to repel Lee's invasion. Above the marching men smoke-colored dust billowed and drifted as their column wound along—a solid mass of dark and light blue punctuated by the steely glint of rifles. Infantrymen helped themselves to the large sweet cherries beside the road as they passed through lush green Maryland farm country with knee-high corn and ripening grain.

Leaving the sometimes hostile state of Maryland and crossing into Pennsylvania, the drum corps struck up "Yankee Doodle," but the inhabitants behind their roadside stands selling bread, milk, cakes, and pies did not respond to this patriotic gesture. Seeing this, many of the hungry men, outraged at the prices, began to help themselves.

"Thieving Rebels!" angry vendors shouted at them. It was the worst insult they could think of. The Union troops ignored them. But the farther north they went, the friendlier people became and the lower the prices.

Nearing Hanover, Pennsylvania, that afternoon, they had a shock. All around lay dead horses and Union cavalrymen with eyes staring upward as though they had seen a sight too horrible to tell. What had happened? Confederate general Jeb Stuart had been through here with a large force of cavalry and skirmished briefly as he passed. The audacious Stuart, emerging from the Blue Ridge Mountains, had galloped boldly around the entire Federal army, past its right flank, proceeding to sever all telegraph lines linking General Meade to his high headquarters in Washington.

Late that afternoon a tired Colonel Chamberlain and his men bivouacked just outside Hanover, and the colonel

Gettysburg, Pennsylvania

sat alone, grateful for fresh bread and milk from one of the vendors. What a surprising life he was leading! A graduate of a theological seminary, his only training in supervision had been to run a Sunday school and teach at Bowdoin College. Now thirty-three, he saw soldiering as a romantic adventure. It was downright un-Christian for a man trained for the ministry, he thought with some chagrin.

Watching curiously as a rider, his horse lathered, rode up to brigade commander Ames, he knew it was bad news. The First and Eleventh Corps had run into Lee at a town to the west called Gettysburg. General Reynolds had been killed, and Confederates had pursued the First Corps into town. Union soldiers not taken prisoner were dug in on some hills on the Hanover side of Gettysburg waiting for help. In July, 1863, there were only twenty-four hundred residents in Gettysburg, but the little town was at the center of a network of ten important roads—two leading west to passes in South Mountain, others to Harrisburg, Baltimore, and nearby towns. Some were meandering farm roads rambling over ridges or encircling the bases of scattered granite hills.

Shoving the rest of the homemade bread in his haversack, Chamberlain ordered his tired men to break camp and march. Gettysburg was a dozen miles to the west. In three days—from July 1 to July 3, 1863—more than one hundred seventy thousand men would shoot, knife, grapple, and kill each other here until pools of blood stood in the small depressions upon the rocks.

Chamberlain himself rode at the head of the column, his well-muscled body erect, a striking man with finely shaped head and classic profile, his dashing moustache

A *Mystic Power at Gettysburg*

swept back from the upper lip. Overhead, the moon rose, and when it was not concealed by the clouds, both soldiers and the Pennsylvania countryside were washed in pale golden light. Along winding, rutted roads, through forests, across fields, and past an occasional farm house, they marched in silence.

And if the minds of these men from Maine sometimes turned homeward, it was to dream of white farm houses and coastal villages, gulls wheeling over blue water and stony shores, fishing boats bobbing on tossing waves, sequestered forests with axes ringing in the cold winter dawn, oxen and stocky farm horses laboring to drag gleaming plow blades through stony earth, and the scent of lilacs in the spring.

Spurs constantly led off the road the two colonels had agreed was the most direct. But finally, when they knew they must be getting close to Gettysburg, they came to what appeared to be an important fork. Here the Twentieth Maine halted while the officers debated over which direction to take.

Suddenly the clouds parted, and the moon shone down upon a horseman wearing a bright coat and tricorn hat. Mounted on a magnificent pale horse, he cantered down one of the roads branching off before them. Turning slightly toward them, he waved them to follow.

In his later report Chamberlain described the event.

"At a turn of the road a staff officer, with an air of authority, told each colonel as he came up, 'General McClellan is in command again, and he's riding up ahead of us on the road.'

"Men waved their hats, cheered until they were hoarse, and, wild with excitement, followed the figure on horseback. Although weary, they marched with a miraculous enthusiasm believing that their beloved general had returned to lead them into battle."

Soon an awed murmur began to travel from one man to another, back through the ranks of troops. Now a different name was heard.

"It's Washington!" exclaimed the men to each other, passing the magic name along. "General Washington himself come to lead us!" And they followed.

The very air was charged with energy and confidence. Although they had no foreknowledge of where they were going or how the land lay, Chamberlain and his Twentieth Maine were on their way to one of the most strategic positions in the coming battle.

When Chamberlain's men arrived at the edge of a wheatfield, they waited, gathered for instructions. Before them the woods were a fearful sight. They seemed to roar as smoke and fiery bursts of light hovered over treetops. Beneath the men's feet the ground shuddered from bursts of artillery.

Meanwhile Union general Gouverneur K. Warren had ridden to the summit of a hill called Little Round Top. It was a large granite outcropping, and he found it completely undefended. Gazing down at the land around him with the eye of a military engineer and strategist, Warren foresaw its importance. On impulse he sent word to a battery below to fire a shot into the woods. It had its effect. The projectile above the trees caused the ranks of Confederates who were concealed in the forest to look up. When they did, their shifting bayonets caught the rays of the sun and reflected hundreds of flashes of light visible to the Union general.

A Mystic Power at Gettysburg

General Warren thought about the line in Byron's poem about the Assyrians: "And the sheen of their spears was like stars on the sea when the blue wave rolls nightly on deep Galilee."

He was badly shocked by the enemy's numbers. So long was the Confederate battle line that it could easily outflank the Union left. It would enable General Longstreet and his men to capture Little Round Top. Warren saw the hill as the key to victory. He immediately sent for help, and Colonel Chamberlain's men were in the ideal position to respond quickly.

There was no easy approach to this ugly rock-strewn mound of stone called Little Round Top. Colonel Strong Vincent started toward the northwest slope, but he found the rock side too rough to mount. He and Chamberlain skirted the base of the hill, conferred, and decided to go up through some woods. Vincent, followed by Chamberlain, began scrambling up the incline. By now the Confederates realized what was happening and were sweeping the lower part of the hill with artillery fire. Colonel Chamberlain's three sons were riding abreast near him. Two of them had come to help the chaplain and ambulance men.

When a large projectile whizzed past, Chamberlain said, "Boys, I don't like this. Another shot might make it hard for your mother." He ordered one of his sons to the rear of the regiment to keep it well closed and sent the other ahead to prepare a place for the wounded.

First to charge the Twentieth Maine was the 4th Alabama—lean, fierce men crouched among the rocks. The smoke of their gunfire spread across the Twentieth Maine's entire front. No sooner had the attack begun

Gettysburg, Pennsylvania

than a lieutenant spied a mass of Confederates vastly outnumbering the Twentieth Maine advancing toward their flank. It was to be only the first of a multitude of tactical problems they would have.

The great dilemma came in less than two hours. The Twentieth Maine had only sixty rounds per man. They had fired almost every round, and for a short time there was a lull. Colonel Chamberlain stood off alone thinking. His men would be slaughtered here . . . and so would he.

Meanwhile, across the valley, a Confederate soldier saw the solitary Union officer with a flowing black mustache standing just behind the center of the lines of the Twentieth Maine. From the man's demeanor, the Confederate knew he must be either the general or an extremely important commander. To steady his rifle the soldier rested his rifle upon a large rock. Viewing his human target over the sights, he took aim, but when he started to pull the trigger he felt a strange reluctance to kill the man. He sighted again. This time he was determined to shoot. Once more, to his bewilderment, he was unable to squeeze the trigger.

Now disaster was only minutes away for the Twentieth Maine, and all down the line men's hoarse, frantic voices shouted, "Ammunition! For God's sake! Ammunition!"

Hastily they began to search the bodies around them on the ground. They stripped cartridge boxes off the dead and dying and tore them open in their haste. But there was not enough. Men who had fired their last rounds turned desperately to Chamberlain, who had been considering the alternatives. Ordered to hold the ground at

A Mystic Power at Gettysburg

all costs, they could not withdraw. There just wasn't any good option. Then this colonel, who seemed to have a talent for doing the impossible, stepped forward.

Only surprise might work. The men of the Twentieth Maine heard his commanding voice ring out above the sounds of battle.

"Fix Bayonets! Charge!"

Shocked, for a long, tense moment they didn't move—fishermen, farmers, woodsmen, just ordinary men. They hesitated as men do when facing incredible odds, possibly death. Would they obey?

Suddenly, an imposing figure stood in front of the line exhorting them to follow. The rays of the afternoon sun set his upraised sword aflame. Once more the Twentieth Maine was seized by the same exultation they had felt following the phantom horseman on the road to Little Round Top. *He* was leading them again! Inspired by supernatural bravery they plunged down the hill thrusting their bayonets into the ranks of the amazed Alabamians. Bewildered, the Confederates had no time to fire a decisive volley, and as they fell back their line broke. In spite of courage, weapons, and superior numbers, they fled.

Chamberlain and his Twentieth Maine had performed one of the miracles of the war. Seldom in the annals of history has there been a more baffling defeat.

John Pullen, author of *The Twentieth Maine,* describes it best when he says, "to find any parallel, it would almost be necessary to go back to Second Kings, 7:3, wherein the four leprous men said to one another, 'Why sit we here until we die?' Then they rose up and advanced into the camp of the Syrians, the Lord at the proper mo-

"Fix bayonets!" came the Federal command.
"Charge!" Amazed, the Confederates fell back.

A Mystic Power at Gettysburg

ment causing the Syrians to hear 'a noise of chariots and a noise of horses, even the noise of a great host,' so that the Syrians all fled for their lives."

When General Joshua Chamberlain was an old man, an interviewer asked him, "Is there any truth to the story that your men saw the figure of George Washington leading them at Gettysburg?"

Chamberlain gazed thoughtfully out of the window of his home across the Maine fields, and there was a long pause. Then he nodded.

"Yes, that report was circulated through our lines, and I have no doubt that it had a tremendous psychological effect in inspiring the men. Doubtless it was a superstition, but who among us can say that such a thing was impossible? We have not yet sounded or explored the immortal life that lies out beyond the Bar.

"We know not what mystic power may be possessed by those who are now bivouacking with the dead. I only know the effect, but I dare not explain or deny the cause. I do believe that we were enveloped by the powers of the other world that day and who shall say that Washington was not among the number of those who aided the country that he founded?"

ooo

Some years after the war Chamberlain, who had later become one of the Union army's finest generals, received a letter from the Confederate who had him in his sights during the final moments of the battle of Little Round Top. He said he was glad he had not pulled the trigger!

Fort Monroe—
The fort has been maintained in its original form in the shape of an irregular heptagon and is completely surrounded by a moat. It is the only fort of its kind in the United States. Robert E. Lee, later to become commander of the Army of Northern Virginia, played a prominent part in its construction.

Driving east toward Norfolk or west toward Williamsburg, take exit 268 off Hwy. 64. Then watch for Fort Monroe or Casemate Museum signs.

ᴼᴼᴼ

THE HAUNTINGS AT FORT MONROE

Fort Monroe, Virginia

Most apparitions walk on moonlit nights, but the one in "Ghost Alley" at Fort Monroe walks only when the night is pitch black. Then how does one see this specter? Those who have met her know.

In fact, according to long-time residents at the fort, countless manifestations of the supernatural have occurred here. And, if we are inclined to believe spirit name-droppers, the ghosts of quite a roster of distinguished people have materialized in the buildings.

Fort Monroe was one of the few forts in the South not captured during the Civil War. Completely surrounded by a moat, like castles of yore, the fort is in the shape of a heptagon, its three sides facing the waters of Chesapeake Bay and Hampton Roads. Designed by a former aide to Napoleon, General Simon Bernard, it was the most powerful fort in the country. The three buildings inside the

At Fort Monroe, with its forbidding moat, the ghosts still roam.

fort's walls are the two "Tuileries" and Old Quarters Number One.

During the war there were fourteen hundred residents within the walls of the fort: militia from Massachusetts and Vermont, the New York Volunteers, and a group of German soldiers known as the Steuben Rifles. The atmosphere of Fort Monroe was very much like that of a small town.

A career military man who has been there for more than a decade has no reluctance to talk about the fort's ghosts, some of them still sighted today. "The most famous apparition is at the plantation-style home called Old Quarters Number One," said he. "They say the house is a veritable Who's Who of distinguished ghosts."

Stories about Old Quarters relate that many appari-

Fort Monroe, Virginia

tions have appeared in the room that was once assigned
to guests for freshening up or overnight visits. Some of
the original furniture is still there, and it is a pleasant
room with a cozy fireplace and a window overlooking the
parade ground. Visitors to the house, conducted to this
room for the night, have found a tall gaunt man in a
dressing gown standing before the fireplace with his back
to them, staring into the flames. Startled, the guest usually exits hurriedly, convinced that the figure is that of
President Lincoln, perhaps thinking about his problems
with Confederate ironclads. General Ulysses S. Grant
has also been seen in the house, for it was here that he
is said to have outlined the final Union campaign sealing
the South's defeat at Appomattox.

But what about the specter who has been reported in
Ghost Alley on dark nights? That is a long story, and it
is told by an officer who has some surprising firsthand
information about the participants, long since dead.

In the officer's words, "Our story begins during the
first years of the Civil War with the marriage of a viva-
cious young Virginia girl to a captain at Fort Monroe.
He was incredibly dull and stodgy, and the girl, whom I
know only by the name of Camille, was in every way his
opposite—beautiful, intelligent with just a touch of the
flirt about her—utterly charming.

"Captain Wilhelm Kirtz was gray-haired, somewhat
pompous and considerably older than Camille. He understood her surprisingly well, even warning himself that she
was none too stable, but he was convinced that his greater
maturity would have a 'settling influence' upon the young
woman. He had not reckoned on the problem that he had

The Hauntings at Fort Monroe

always had with jealousy. From the day they were married he watched her, kept track of every outing, even those with other women on the post, and lived in constant dread that she would fall in love with someone else.

"Their social circle at Fort Monroe was a small one where it was almost impossible for the officers and their wives not to see each other daily, and what some might have described as 'her flirtations' were not serious. Now and then they earned her the dagger-like glares of a few of the wives, but nothing ever came of them. If there was any unseemly conduct, it was on the part of certain foolish husbands for, to be fair to her, the captain's wife never behaved with any impropriety. Yet his dread of losing her love obsessed him.

"He was prone to sudden jealous rages, often accusing her cruelly and sometimes even beating her while she cried out piteously, protesting her innocence. On several occasions there was gossip about marks on her arms or a shoulder when her gown slipped to bare a little more of the smooth white skin than would normally be revealed. But despite this her conduct remained blameless.

"Then a handsome young officer arrived at the fort, and the women with marriageable daughters made much over him. A Frenchman, he was a fine figure of a man with flowing blond mustaches and sparkling blue eyes. His gaze was often upon the ladies, but soon he seemed to watch only one in particular. The mothers noticed, and the daughters themselves were furious that this most eligible single man should pay his attentions to a married woman, but the husband, who usually worried over everything, seemed completely unaware that there might be the beginning of a romance between Camille and Pierre.

Fort Monroe, Virginia

"Camille, habitually berated and struck by her husband, was comforted by the Frenchman's attentions and did not realize the depth of her feeling for him. Actually, with so little opportunity for them to be alone on the post, these feelings would probably have passed had it not been for one event.

"Finally Captain Kirtz was summoned by his superior officer and sent to Richmond on a special mission. He was ordered to take a message to the commanding general of the city, but the stodgy captain suspected that the message was not particularly serious but rather an excuse to send him to shop for the post commandant's favorite delicacies. He knew the commandant's taste for luxury. Moreover he knew that the commandant would soon be entertaining an important general. Musing about all this, he decided the errand was not in keeping with his dignity or rank.

"While Kirtz was gone the weather was cloudy and at night the moon did not show itself. The darkest street on the post was a narrow alley named Matthews Street, and it was here that Pierre persuaded Camille to meet him. His attractiveness and her indignation over her husband's abuse were so great that they overcame her customary discretion, and she agreed. The pair were alone for the first time, and before they parted Camille believed herself to be deeply in love. But this was too dangerous a meeting place. They might easily be seen by some of the residents of the street, and so Pierre soon boldly visited her quarters.

"Meanwhile the Captain delivered his message to the commanding general in Richmond, and, irritated over this demeaning mission, he speedily completed his purchase and was on his way back to the fort.

The Hauntings at Fort Monroe

"He returned late at night, a full day before he was expected, and finding his wife and Pierre in a lovers' embrace, he drew his pistol and shot. The sound was heard and officers hurried into the building from nearby quarters, in various stage of undress, to find Camille seriously wounded. Someone summoned a physician. Whether he had intended to shoot Pierre and, in his emotional state, had shot his wife instead is unknown, but in the confusion Pierre escaped. Camille moaned and repeated the young Frenchman's name over and over coupled with terms of endearment that doubtless increased her husband's rage.

"'Oh Pierre, my dear Pierre!'—the words could still be heard as her husband, taken into custody, was led away. One of the women bathed Camille's wound where the bullet had entered below her left breast, while a shocked crowd watched the captain emerging, under guard, into the street below. Camille died that morning. Kirtz was not executed for his wife's murder, because of the circumstances in which he had found her, but neither was he freed. He was made to serve a prison sentence, although no one has ever agreed upon how long it was.

"Now for the most amazing aspect of the case.

"Years later a letter found in a Richmond lockbox came into my possession. Faded and stained with tears, it was in a man's handwriting and made such an impression on me that I believe I know it by heart. This is the wording of the letter:

I had been gone for many years, but on Saturday last, I returned to Fort Monroe for the first time since my crime. A very kind young officer urged me to share his quarters, and I accepted. I did not give my

Fort Monroe, Virginia

real name to the fellow but rather that of an officer who had been a comrade at the Fort.

That night I was too full of painful memories and guilt to sleep, and I decided to walk. Hands clasped behind me, deep in thought, I found myself strolling along Matthews Street—a street that was always so pitch dark I wondered why I had chosen it. As I walked I noticed ahead of me a soft glow upon the street such as that emitted from the light of a lantern but I saw no one. When I realized the cause I was too terrified to cry out. Before me stood Camille, as lovely as she had been in life, but instead of the white wraith-like form that I had always associated with apparitions, her limbs and clothing possessed a peculiar and blinding sheen. I placed both hands over my eyes and fell to my knees in the middle of the alleyway.

"Camille! Camille! Forgive me," I said in a choking voice barely able to speak. She did not reply; but it seemed to me I heard her give a long, tremulous sigh. I remember every detail—my body trembling, the autumn breeze tossing dead leaves from the road about her feet, the anguish in her face. And her form—I can only describe it as luminous, pulsating from soft diffuseness to extreme brightness. I knew instantly that it was Camille, and despite her sin, all I have been able to think about was every blow that I gave her during our marriage—how I made her days miserable, and, perhaps, brought about the very event I so dreaded.

God forgive me!

Wilhelm Kirtz"

After the officer had finished his story we were both

silent for a while, and then I asked, "How do you happen to be familiar with so many details of the story? Could they have come from Captain Kirtz's descendants?"

"Not really. My great-grandfather was the man with whom Kirtz had stayed at the post at the time he wrote the letter, and they became friends. He had no idea of his guest's identity until after the captain died, and it was then he found himself the captain's sole heir. Actually, he had been left a great deal in gold which the lonely, shunned man wanted him to have as a token of his gratitude for their friendship. Along with personal mementos was the tragic letter. There seems to have been no clue to the captain's profession after he was released from prison. And now I have told you all I know of the apparition of the luminous lady."

Other supernatural phenomena happened at Fort Monroe during the decade of the 1980s, according to a museum staff member.

"An incident that has been much discussed occurred when an extremely agitated woman, a newcomer who had moved into one of the houses at the fort, burst into the museum asking a staff member's explanation for a strange event she had just witnessed.

"In her own words, 'My two children and I were watching a Barbara Walters interview on television when something very frightening occurred. A Victorian table with a heavy marble top went sailing across the room landing in the fireplace with a crash. The marble was broken, but the Waterford crystal lamp that had stood in the center of the table landed undamaged and upright on the floor!'

"It was some time before the woman could be calmed.

Fort Monroe, Virginia

In fact she was trembling. The house where the table flew across the room was in a section of old homes in the fort inside the moat. The one in which the marble top table sailed across the room is near another where a few years ago workmen reported an unusual experience. They were engaged in some work in the attic, and after completing repairs, one of them made a comment to the lady of the house: 'Your little boy sat watching us, and he colored so quietly with his crayons the entire time that he didn't bother us at all. You certainly have a good child.'

"'But we have no children!' exclaimed the astonished woman. Later she discovered that some years before a child who had once lived in the house had met a sudden, rather dreadful death."

As a place where history has been made for over three hundred and sixty years, it is not surprising that Fort Monroe is still reported to be haunted. Captain John Smith, who commented on it as a fine site for a castle, Lafayette, Lincoln, Jefferson Davis, U. S. Grant, and Edgar Allan Poe are only a few of the famous who are still said to make spectral appearances.

And then there are specters of ordinary people like the rest of us—the unidentified little boy who managed to leave the afterlife briefly and materialize just long enough to shock the living.

But none is able to match the stunning effect of the Luminous Lady of Ghost Alley.

Harpers Ferry—
Harpers Ferry was an important Civil War military objective for both North and South. Located at the head of the Shenandoah Valley, it was considered the gateway to the South. It was the site of an arsenal, an armory, and a rifle works. Original buildings are much as they were at the time of the Civil War, conveying a unique, almost eerie atmosphere. The Potomac and Shenandoah Rivers meet at the foot of the town.

Harpers Ferry National Historical Park is located on
U.S. Route 340 at Harpers Ferry, West Virginia.

○○○

THE MAN WHO WON'T STAY DEAD

Harpers Ferry, West Virginia

His bright blue eyes watched Ed Coppoc intently, until finally he reached for the knife-tipped pike in Coppoc's hand. "This is the right way to do it," he said, holding the blade at about a ten-degree angle with his left hand and grasping the stone with his right. Almost lovingly he rhythmically stroked the blade away from him. When, on each side, he could feel the blade catch the fleshy part of his thumb, he knew that the long knife was sharp— sharp as a razor's edge. Only then did he hand it back.

"Think we're goin' to need this many of 'em, sir?" asked Coppoc, looking at the stack of over a thousand pikes leaning against the wall of the farmhouse. The two men sat side by side on the porch, legs dangling off the edge.

"I had the blacksmith make a plenty of them because the Negroes will need to arm themselves." Brown's thin

Harpers Ferry, West Virginia

lips were tightly compressed. "If citizens interfere, I must burn the town and have blood."

It was October 16, 1859, at the Kennedy Farmhouse across the river from Harpers Ferry where John Brown and his followers had been secretly gathering. Even on this momentous day he did not deviate from his ritual. The tall bearded man read a chapter in the Bible to his followers and said a short prayer, standing while he prayed. He seldom knelt—even before God. While the men made preparations, he spent most of his time pacing back and forth on the long porch that stretched across the front of the house or walking out in the yard.

Late that afternoon he looked at the eighteen men around him and muttered to himself, "Plenty of arms and ammunition—we're ready to go." Aloud, he added, "Men, put on your arms; we will proceed to the Ferry."

With these words John Brown, self-dubbed "Commander-in-Chief," ordered his "troops" into action. Wagons filled with pikes, fagots, sledgehammers, and crowbars pulled up to the farmhouse door. The men, whom Brown himself had commissioned, were finally on their way to free the slaves. Around their shoulders the gray shawls that served them in lieu of coats had the look of shrouds. Thrusting his battle-worn old Kansas cap down on his head, Brown hoisted himself up on the wagon seat.

From the first moment he had seen the town of Harpers Ferry he had seen it as a castle upon a hill—a castle that he would storm and make his. The encircling rivers were the moat. The only approaches to the town were two bridges, one across the Shenandoah, the other across the Potomac. He had chosen the Maryland bridge across

The Man Who Won't Stay Dead

the Potomac. It was six miles to the bridge, and in the misty, gloomy night they could see little. They heard the creak of the wagon wheels and the soft, continual thud of their own feet marching.

Meanwhile in Canada, Harriet Tubman, whom John Brown had asked for help, was having a dream. Dreams often guided her. When she awoke from this one she was filled with foreboding. She sympathized with his goal, but she had her own—rescuing slaves from the South and getting them safely to freedom in Canada. Her mission was already a success.

Of the group of raiders, only the commander John Brown believed that the assault on the U.S. Arsenal at Harpers Ferry would accomplish his purpose. He had held this view as far back as 1854, when he was in Kansas. Yet, even as he and his men were approaching the sleeping town, this strange leader had no definite campaign plan, no well-defined purpose other than to attack and capture the arsenal, arm the slaves, and terrify the people of Virginia. According to his son Salmon, Brown changed his mind about the details of the raid several times, even up until the last few minutes before he and his men entered the town.

He finally decided to capture a couple of slaveholders as hostages, at the same time rallying the slaves who would follow him to the other side of the Potomac. There he would arm them, and with him and his men they would flee to the Virginia mountains. The military way of doing all this would have been first to establish a mountain camp, then to swoop down upon the town swiftly and spread terror across the state, and, finally, to stay only briefly in the town, leaving for their mountain fastness within an hour or two.

Brown sent a man named Aaron Stevens and four armed raiders with torches to break into the home of Colonel Lewis Washington about midnight and inform him that he was their prisoner. The colonel was President Washington's great-grandnephew, and he had inherited a sword that had been a gift to the president from Frederick the Great. Obeying the express order of John Brown, Stevens first demanded that Washington present the famous sword to the black raider Osborn Anderson. Symbolism had always been important to Brown and he thought this gesture was symbolic.

In the wagon Washington's slaves huddled around him, nervous and bewildered. Stevens stopped next at the house of a slave owner named John Allstadt. He heaved a fence rail through the front door, and the sharp crash and splintering wood waked the family. Allstadt and his son were led outside at gunpoint and ordered into the family's four-horse wagon along with their six black slaves.

As the wagons rolled into Harpers Ferry, someone asked, "Why is everything so quiet? Is everyone in town killed?" No one answered. At daybreak the hostages were taken into the armory fire-engine house.

Raiders entering Harpers Ferry earlier had shot at the bridge night watchman, but tragically the first man they mortally wounded was the baggagemaster, Shephard Hayward. He was a free black who had gone to find out why the 1:00 A.M. passenger train was late. Hayward knew the raiders as friends who had been in Harpers

The Man Who Won't Stay Dead

Ferry often, and he did not stop when he saw them approach. They shot him and he ran. Lying in agony from the pain of his wound, he died in the railroad station twelve hours later.

Brown buckled the elaborate sword of President Washington around his waist. He was to wear it throughout the ensuing ordeal. Stevens introduced "Captain Brown" to Colonel Washington.

Glancing with contempt at the stolen sword hanging from Brown's waist but not commenting upon it, Washington said, "Ossawatomie," calling Brown by the name he had been given after he, his five sons, and three other men had massacred five slavery sympathizers at Potawatomie, Kansas. They had shot James P. Boyle, hacked his two sons and a man named Allen Wilkinson to death with short swords, and the fifth, William Sherman, they killed and threw into the river.

"Yes, I'm Ossawatomie Brown of Kansas," said the commander of the raiders. He then demanded Washington's watch and silver money, claiming that "this is not plunder to enrich ourselves but an act to appropriate the property of slaveholders."

Suddenly Brown's mind flashed back to the hostages in Kansas whom he and his sons had brutally hacked to death. He recalled their pleas, the asinine prayers before they died. What sinners! The Lord wouldn't spare men like that. But their deaths hadn't changed the situation.

This must be different, Brown thought, *an event that will change history.* His hostages, both white and black, were already inside the armory fire-engine house. Better tell the black men what to do, he thought, and he thrust a pike into the hands of each. Each pike had a handle

Harpers Ferry, West Virginia

like a pitchfork. At one end was a wicked iron blade shaped like a butcher knife.

"Take these," he said pushing them toward the slave hostages, "and don't let the other prisoners get off the pavement."

Some said later that the slaves would put the spears to one side and pick them up if they saw Brown coming. Raider Stevens threatened their buttocks with the blade if they laid their weapons down. "He was a mean devil," according to young Allstedt. As it grew light raiders began grabbing anybody who passed the engine house and taking them prisoner.

Inside Brown looked around him. When he had started out on this raid there were twenty-two men in all. Six were members of his family or connected by marriage, five were black men. He paced back and forth waiting for reinforcements. He was getting restless and beginning to experience some anxiety, but Captain John Cook kept reassuring him.

"The slaves are on the way. You've got nothing to worry about." The harsh lines of worry on Brown's face softened a little.

"Black people from this whole area are going to be gathering here soon," predicted Cook. Brown was growing elated, certain his dream of the blacks gathering under his leadership to fight for their freedom was coming true. But Cook had not done as much notifying as he pretended he had, and the blacks of the area had more training in obedience and in following men they knew. No volunteers arrived.

By morning everyone in the engine house was hungry, and Brown sent his son Oliver and one of the hostages

The Man Who Won't Stay Dead

to get food. It was only a short distance. He didn't think anyone would shoot because of the danger of harming the prisoner. The pair had just set out when a boy at the engine house pointed to an upper window in a tavern, yelling "Look! Those two men are going to shoot them!"

Oliver Brown and his hostage carried a makeshift flag. It is not clear whether they hoped to bring back food from the Wager House hotel or whether this was a flag of truce to encourage bargaining, although the older Brown would agree to nothing other than complete freedom for his raiders. The prisoner escaped, but young Brown was hit. Although he was seriously wounded, he managed to drag himself back to the engine house. He died several hours later.

From within Brown looked out to see a lone figure walking casually along the railroad trestle. It was Colonel Beckham, the popular mayor of Harpers Ferry who also served as stationmaster. He was unarmed. A long platform extended from the depot beside the Potomac. Beckham reached the water tank and peered around the end. Edwin Coppoc fired.

"Did you git him?" Brown asked.

"No. But if he peeks again I'll make sure of him by letting my bullet nip a corner of the tank." The mayor looked out and Coppoc fired. Beckham died instantly, his body tumbling from behind the tank and sprawling grotesquely upon the platform.

By now the engine house was jammed with men—too many for such a small space. Brown's big black dog with a white stripe on his face and white paws was continually underfoot. The townspeople could easily have captured the engine house, for there were only six raiders inside.

Harpers Ferry, West Virginia

Brown didn't worry. He knew they wouldn't want to hurt Washington, the young Allstedt boy, and the other hostages. Bullets were flying around the small building sporadically, their purpose more to keep Brown from coming out than to kill the people inside.

Brown's son Watson looked out the door through his gun sites at a man just opposite him. The man had seen him, too. But Watson didn't shoot quite quickly enough, and the other's bullet struck him.

"For God's sake kill me! Put me out of my suffering," Watson said to his father, and he went on pleading with him half the night.

"Quit your noise and die like a man," came the abrupt reply.

Toward morning Brown called to his son and got no answer.

"Guess he's dead," Brown said to no one in particular.

After Watson was shot the raiders barred the door and pushed one of the fire engines up against it. The hostages huddled together, quiet and frightened. They could hear men shouting outside, and the occasional shooting discouraged them from attempting to get out. The inside of the engine house was dark as a dungeon. Hostages lay on the brick floor or sat up against the wall half asleep from exhaustion.

Sometime during the early morning hours a company of United States Marines arrived from Washington under the command of Lieutenant Colonel Robert E. Lee. About mid-morning Lieutenant J. E. B. Stuart came to the engine house door and twice asked Brown to surrender.

The Man Who Won't Stay Dead

"I ain't a–goin' to do it."

"I've got ninety men out here and I'll make you do it," Stuart said.

"All right," replied Brown and shut the door.

The marines began battering down the door with sledges and a heavy ladder while the raiders fired at them out of the portholes, killing one marine and wounding another. The prisoners within were filled with fear.

Marine lieutenant Green dashed inside first. Brown was about to shoot him when the officer cut at him with his saber, hitting Brown's gun up in the air so that the bullet went over the lieutenant's head. Green's next stroke knocked Brown down. At this Coppoc and the other raiders threw down their guns and surrendered, except for one who jumped up shouting, "I'm a citizen prisoner."

"Oh no you aren't!" said an officer, grasping the man's arm and taking him along with the other prisoners. Brown himself couldn't walk. The marines laid him on the grass and stood in a circle around him, bayonets fixed, to keep the crowd from harming him.

"Stand back. Get back there!" the marines shouted at angry onlookers. Finally the train arrived and the raiders were taken to jail in Charlestown, eight miles south of Harpers Ferry, where they would be tried.

Convicted and sentenced to be hanged, on December 2, 1859, Brown left his prison cell for the last time. He handed this prophetic message to someone who stood near the scaffold.

I John Brown am now quite *certain* that the crimes of the *guilty land will* never be purged *away* but with

Harpers Ferry, West Virginia

Blood. I had as I now *think: vainly* flattered myself
that without *very* much bloodshed it might be done.

Colonel J. T. L. Preston, present at the hanging, wrote:
"the man of strong and bloody hand, of fierce passions,
of iron will, of wonderful vicissitudes,—the terrible par-
tisan of Kansas—the capturer of the United States Arsenal at Harpers Ferry—the would-be Catiline of the
South—the demigod of the Abolitionists—the man exe-
crated and lauded—damned and prayed for ... John
Brown was hanging between heaven and earth."

The presence of John Brown's strong personality pervades Harpers Ferry, and perhaps that is why some say
that he has never really left the town.

Stories of supernatural appearances abound. One of
the most often heard is that tourists see a tall stern
bearded man who looks strikingly like Brown. They stop
him, mention his remarkable resemblance to Brown, almost apologetically, and then ask if he will do them the
favor of posing with members of the family in a picture.
When the film is developed the man who was the very
image of Brown is not there.

Others report watching a man who looks exactly like
Brown walk along in front of the old storefronts with a
large black dog at his side. When they reach the fire-
engine house both vanish through the closed door!

Some say Harpers Ferry *is* John Brown. His strong presence
pervades this town.

OOOO

Vicksburg—
On July 4, 1863, following the siege of Vicksburg, General John Clifford Pemberton surrendered the city that had been considered "the impregnable fortress," together with his army of almost thirty thousand men, to General Ulysses S. Grant and his army of seventy-seven thousand. This campaign ensured Grant's reputation as one of the great generals in U.S. military history.

Vicksburg National Military Park is on U.S. 61 at Vicksburg, Mississippi.

OOO

THE HAUNTING OF MCRAVEN

Vicksburg, Mississippi

Music could be heard, first faintly in the distance, then bands blaring "Yankee Doodle." Banners were streaming and beneath them were officers in blue uniforms, their horses prancing proudly.

As the Union Army marched toward the city emaciated Confederate soldiers streamed through Vicksburg streets. "Nothing but starvation whipped us"—the comment could be heard on all sides. Residents, some of whom had lived in caves near the battle lines but beneath hills that sheltered them from the Union bombardment, hurried back to their homes to wait with apprehension.

Ragged Southern troops stood in pathetic groups on the streets, and, as the men began to mix, there was praise from the victors for the "wonderful defense." Some of the Union soldiers began taking bread from their own haversacks and sharing it with the hungry Confeder-

90

ates—the former enemy whom they had been engaged in "starving out" only a few days before.

But this is a story about a house named McRaven.

Just after Union troops entered the city, John Bobb, the owner of McRaven, an imposing home with double verandas built in 1791, found soldiers vandalizing his magnificent boxwood and magnolia gardens. Recklessly, he ordered them off his property and for this was shot through the heart. To General Grant's credit, the soldiers were court martialed, but it was not the last tragic occurrence at McRaven.

In the early days of the occupation Colonel Wilson and Captain McPherson were walking about the city when Wilson paused at the entrance to the imposing Greek Revival house at 1445 Harrison Street. He stared at it admiringly. Seeing his interest, McPherson suggested they headquarter there. The house had interested McPherson when he lived in the city. In a sense this was a homecoming, finding himself back walking the streets of Vicksburg. When he left, he had not known whether he would live to see the city again or not. Perhaps he would be shot before he reached the Federal lines, but he had been lucky.

From those early days of the siege McPherson had served the Yankee colonel. The pair had been aboard a Yazoo River steamer, and a strong friendship had developed between them. McPherson would continue to prove his usefulness during the occupation, thought Wilson; the captain knew the people's ways well, but the colonel did not.

Vicksburg, Mississippi

McPherson, a tall blue-eyed Scot with curly brown hair and a slight burr to his words, was a single man whose family lived in Illinois. He had moved to Vicksburg a few years ago, and because of his Northern sympathies soon deserted to the Union. Settlers from all over the country and Europe had come down the Mississippi, and some had made a fortune at this trading center on the great river.

The house was cool despite the summer heat, and each day Colonel Wilson gave the captain orders to transmit to staff. Townspeople who wished to curry favor brought vegetables, poultry, or fish, asking exorbitant prices, but the sergeant in charge of the kitchen bought. The men did not want to eat hardtack, and there was little on store shelves. In the house McPherson had discovered a cache of fine liquors which they served when entertaining other officers. Sometimes they held gala parties. The young women McPherson had known before he left were markedly cool, and he saw the contempt in their eyes, but he found others eager to accept invitations to parties at McRaven after the austerity of the siege.

It was a relief to the colonel to have McPherson take care of so many things. He even performed the function of tour guide, conducting visiting Federal officers around the city, explaining its history. One day Wilson and McPherson visited the caves beneath the bluff where many people had lived during the shelling of the city. Wilson was amazed at what deprivation they must have endured under siege. Of course, he could look at the emaciated men on the streets, men who still wore remnants of Confederate uniforms and stayed on, not happily but because they had nowhere else to go. Vicksburg was home.

The Haunting of McRaven

And then there were the hungry children. Some no longer had fathers, or if they did those fathers were having difficulty feeding their families. The captain adored children and always saw to it that they were brought biscuits and sometimes cookies to eat from McRaven's kitchen. "I don't want the next generation to grow up hating us like this one does," he would tell the colonel.

Rebuilding and other measures to restore the city to a more livable state began. Sometimes Colonel Wilson would stop to speak to a worker loading rubble from a shelled building and discover, to his surprise, that he was speaking to a man of education and culture. Occasionally it was someone McPherson had known personally, and when the tall blue-eyed McPherson in his Union officer's uniform was recognized, it was usually embarrassing. After the first flash of recognition, the icy stare in response to his greeting contained real hatred. In some respects this occupation duty was a lonely task for both men.

Wilson thought often of his wife and his seventeen-year-old daughter, Elizabeth. When McPherson was unaware, his superior officer would gaze thoughtfully at him. If they both survived the war, McPherson, on his way to Illinois, might travel back with him through western Maryland and stop over at his home. He liked the captain, and the possibility of a romance between this young man and Elizabeth—the idea of having him as a son-in-law—was pleasant to dwell upon. He saw McPherson's warmth toward a little boy named Andrew who came up each day for food, and he liked the captain the better for his compassion.

One night McPherson went to visit some officer

Vicksburg, Mississippi

friends in another regiment. He did not return at his usual hour, and to Wilson's surprise he was not about the next morning. This was so completely unlike his friend that the colonel sent two men to scour the city. Inquiring after McPherson and describing his appearance, they received only shakes of the head and blank looks. By evening the colonel had caused an alert with a full description of Captain McPherson to be issued throughout the city to all of the occupying forces.

A week went by and there was no word of the missing Federal officer. Wilson looked himself, accompanied by Murdoch Steed, a friend of McPherson's. They combed the city, covering every street and quarter except one of the black neighborhoods. Finally they searched that area.

"No suh. Ain't seen him," was the usual answer. Then someone, staring thoughtfully in the direction of the Mississippi, added, "Co'se they's always the ribbuh." And that was true. A body thrown in its swift waters might never be found and identified. But Colonel Wilson would not give up the search. He extended it to the entire Vicksburg area and offered a reward.

A few weeks later he waked one night, certain he had heard a sound. He lay there and listened, but all was silent. Then he thought he heard it again—the faintest rustle of movement over near the curtain. Fumbling for the candle holder, he lighted the kerosene lamp from the candle's flame. No one was there, and he lay back in the high four poster bed. The loss of McPherson who had become a comrade and whom he had thought of as a possible son-in-law had upset him deeply. As a result, he had been sleeping poorly.

The Haunting of McRaven

He got up and checked the lock of the bedroom door. It was secure as he had left it, and this was a second-floor bedroom. Pushing aside the velvet drapes, the colonel stared down from the high window. The yard below was empty in the moonlight. Adjusting the wick of the lamp so that the flame was low, he did not turn it off. He closed his eyes and tried to get back to sleep. Outside the window he heard the low, mournful howl of a dog. What was it his father used to say? "Howling dogs are an omen of death." He shivered slightly, although he really didn't consider himself superstitious. It was two hours after midnight.

He put his head back upon the plump feather pillow, thinking he really must get some sleep. He had almost dozed off when he heard a noise again—just a squirrel somewhere in the walls or attic of the old house, he told himself, and he kept his eyes shut. Then, as if the heavy door to the hall had opened wide, he felt a draft of cold air—a draft so strong that even through his closed eyelids he knew that the flame of the kerosene lamp had suddenly flickered and almost gone out.

Chill bumps rose on his bare arms. He was not just going to lie there helpless, whatever this was! Putting on a light cotton robe, he seized a rocking chair, turned it to face the door to the hall, and sat down. Perhaps thirty minutes passed. He started to doze off when he felt the chair rocking slightly beneath him. Someone was standing behind him gently pushing it back and forth!

The colonel leaped from the chair in one motion. Wide awake, he saw a tall figure standing between the windows and the chair. It was that of an officer and at first appeared so real that he was outraged to think one of his staff had the disrespect to enter his bedroom. The man stood close enough to touch Wilson, and what a sight he was!

His uniform had been almost torn off, and his head—good God!—how savagely battered! One side of his face was mutilated beyond recognition, but from the other side the shocked Wilson recognized the man immediately. It was Captain McPherson—or had been.

McPherson tried to speak. "No use—don't search further." The colonel saw to his horror that this figure out of a nightmare appeared to be drenched with water. Frightened as he was, Wilson managed to protest. "But we must look. I'll have you," he stammered, "your body sent home."

"No—never find me—the river," he said.

"Who did this to you?"

"Former Confederates. Led by . . ." and McPherson recognized the name of the son of one of Vicksburg's most prominent families.

Trembling with anger he exclaimed, "We'll get him!"

The apparition was greatly agitated. "No!" he burst out to the colonel's surprise. "That would cause trouble between townspeople and troops. . . . *Please.*" His voice was now very weak. Wilson compassionately extended his hand to him, and when he did the tall form began to fade.

The colonel paced the floor in a quandary. He was tempted to go to the Vicksburg aristocrat's home himself and accuse his son of the murder. The killer was a Confederate officer who had surrendered when the city fell. The next morning he would see the commanding Federal officer for the entire city and tell him the story. Would

Union troops occupied Vicksburg, and one Federal officer was
particularly hated.

he take it seriously? Somehow he would convince him.
Finally he returned to his bed to toss restlessly. When
he waked, his mind was in a turmoil. Had the captain
been right in urging him not to pursue the murderer?
He left the breakfast table and walked out on the ve-
randa. As he stood thinking, he saw the children coming
up to the house. In the lead was Andrew.

Now the colonel almost lost his calm demeanor. Andrew was the son of the Confederate officer who had been
responsible for McPherson's murder! The officer had
come home without a leg, and he must have despised his
former friend McPherson. Both fury and anguish welled
up inside the colonel. He would bring the one-time Confederate officer to justice anyway! Andrew stood in front
of him looking up, his young face puzzled. The colonel
couldn't trust himself to speak, he was so filled with
anger. The child of the Confederate soldier stretched out
his hand as he always did.

"Will there be a biscuit, today, sir?" At Andrew's polite
request, Colonel Wilson suddenly recalled the captain's
words: "I don't want the next generation to grow up hating us like this one does." Colonel Wilson took a deep
breath and got hold of himself. He told the boy to wait
and he went into the house. He met Mattie the cook in
the hall.

"Take a tray of biscuits out to the children, Mattie,"
he said, and as an afterthought, "Put some molasses on
them, if we have some."

In 1984 architect Leyland French moved into Mc-
Raven knowing that he had found his heart's desire—a
house of beauty and fascinating architectural design

The Haunting of McRaven

with a dramatic history. He had not the slightest interest in apparitions, but French says that in the spring of 1991 the phantoms were so active that "I had to have the house exorcised." He tells this story.

"Right after I bought the house in 1984, a new tour guide was bringing a group through the parlor, and a lady asked her if the piano played. A tourist reached over and touched a chord, but there was no sound. As they stood in the archway to the hall the tour group heard the notes of waltz behind them. The piano had decided to play!

"Last spring it became so bad you could walk into the house and feel the air get thick—an oppressive force, something demonic. This had not been present before, and I firmly believe it was brought in by an outsider. On one occasion a door slammed on my hand and painfully injured it. Last spring I was coming through the parlor, and suddenly I found myself on the floor, shoved to my knees with a push from behind. At this point I moved out until the house could be exorcised.

"Since an Episcopal priest has come and blessed McRaven, the atmosphere here has been a benign one, and no further oppressive influences have been felt. Of course, with the many soldiers who were hospitalized in the house during the war and the many other residents, any one or more of them might have been the cause of the incidents.

"Awed tourists glimpse figures of Civil War soldiers pacing the gallery now and then, but more often the apparitions are seen by the tour guides, who are in the house daily."

Has the ghost of Captain McPherson ever been seen

since he communicated with the colonel? The answer is yes. The bloody specter of the captain has appeared to others in the years since the Civil War. And then there is the middle bedroom which, according to well-known scholar and writer Charles L. Sullivan, is the domain of a spectral lady with long brown hair and a homespun dress.

There is little doubt but that sometimes the phantoms still roam at McRaven.

ooo

McRaven at 1445 Harrison Street, Vicksburg, is open daily for tours.

Brigadier General J. E. B. Stuart and his cavalry, sent by General Robert E. Lee on a reconnoitering mission, took this order beyond what Lee intended. In a magnificent grandstand play, he rode completely around Major General McClellan's Union army near Richmond, June 12–15, 1862.

○○○

No Rites for a Rebel

Near Linney's Corner, Virginia

"I thought you'd find this an interesting place for a picnic, Leslie. A century ago your great-grandfather crossed this stream in J. E. B. Stuart's cavalry."

Leslie Farley's red lips pouted, and she tossed her blonde curls. "Why should I care whether he was here or not, Bill?"

"Oh, I don't know. Just thought you might. The history that happened along the Chickahominy River would fill a book," said Bill Latané. "The night Mrs. Stuart got here, on her way to Richmond, the bridge was out, so they had to detour. Jeb Stuart died from his wound minutes before she arrived."

"And why should I care about all that now?" Leslie was examining her brightly painted fingernails.

"Sometimes I think nothing interests you but nail polish and clothes!" She ignored him.

Edmund Farley and Emma Lou Harrison pulled up behind them in his Studebaker convertible. They appeared more absorbed in each other than in history.

Leslie looked back and then turned to Bill. "I think

the reason you asked Edmund to bring his car, too, is so you could stay out here alone if you wanted to." She jumped out of the car and went back to the other couple.

"Emma Lou, let's go swimming."

"No. The river is too swift and too high to swim in after the rains," said Edmund.

"He's right," said Bill, "and I don't want to test my classroom resuscitation training on you, Leslie." Bill hoped to become a doctor.

"You said the remains of an old Civil War bridge were here along the river somewhere, didn't you, Bill?" Edmund asked.

"I've read that there's more than one bridge, but I don't know just where."

"I'm hungry," interrupted Leslie.

"Yes. What about the sandwiches and champagne? Isn't it time for them?" asked Emma Lou.

"Right!" said Edmund. "Let's spread this tablecloth over near the river. Leslie, produce the wine!"

Sulkily, Leslie began to unpack the chilled wine and silver goblets from the hamper and then sandwiches of paper-thin Virginia ham and pimento cheese, fruit, and lemon tarts.

"I'll bet Stuart's men didn't eat this sumptuously," said Bill, raising one of the goblets to his lips.

"They did after they had raided a Union camp and stocked up," Edmund said. "Yankee general Meade even served his guests champagne for breakfast, and Stuart's men ate all sorts of delicacies after raids."

"Well, one thing I know," said Emma Lou righteously, "Jeb Stuart was a teetotaler, Edmund Farley, and since he's such a hero to you, you ought to remember that."

No Rites for a Rebel

Edmund grimaced and finished off the wine in his silver goblet with a flourish. Leslie's brother was a jovial fellow, but he had a bit of a wild streak.

"Just think," said Bill with awe, "Stuart and his men passed right by here on their ride around McClellan's entire army. What a feat that ride was!" marveled Bill.

Edmund nodded. "Yes. No hotels, no hospitals, no stables where they could change horses—just the enemy and the threat of capture any moment."

"I get tired of all these stories from the past," complained Emma Lou. "No one has even noticed my new dress. I'm going to get grass stains on it if someone doesn't give me something to sit on." Bill rose and gallantly spread his jacket on the grass for her.

"Why, I've noticed it, Emma Lou," said Leslie. "I never saw you wear anything quite that décolleté before. Would you like for me to adjust it some in the back for you, honey? That might keep it from falling down in front," she purred. Emma Lou glared and turned to begin taking the lemon tarts from their box.

Bill was staring out at the river. "Look at that water level and how wide the Chickahominy is along here. I don't think even I could swim a horse across it today."

"My, you're modest," Edmund teased. "Rooney Lee almost drowned trying to swim it somewhere along here."

"Why don't we start eating, so we won't be late?" urged Leslie. "Personally, I want to get back early to rest and dress for the dinner dance tonight."

"We'll all go together, anyway," said her brother.

While they ate, Edmund and Bill decided that the Confederacy might have won the war if Lee had heeded Stuart's bold letter to take the offensive. The letter was

Near Linney's Corner, Virginia

written right after Lee took command of the army. Edmund ranted about how the military meddling of President Jefferson Davis and General Braxton Bragg's failure to support Fort Fisher had lost the war.

By now the girls were plainly bored. The rest of a warm day lay ahead with no romantic opportunities—no swings for them to be pushed in by the men, no paddleboats in which to race and flirt and challenge each other—none of all the pleasures available in a city park. Worst of all they were beset by bees, attracted by the fragrance of the young women's hair. The insects' chief desire seemed to be to entangle themselves in their long tresses.

"Hateful thing—get away!" Emma Lou screamed at a bumble bee. Then she turned to Leslie. "We would have had a better time in town. Out here the dead get more attention than we do!" She turned to Edmund. "You all talk about the Civil War as if it happened yesterday."

"Well, not yesterday but maybe the day before," Edmund admitted grudgingly. "My grandfather describes the generals, and when I hear him it's like they're in the next room, and maybe, someday, I'll get to meet them.

"We really didn't mean to ignore you," he went on, realizing the girl's pride was hurt. "They were your ancestors too."

Bill spoke up. "As their descendants, we're the ones they were fighting for in a way, Emma—those of us who would be coming after them. This was our country. If you don't care anything about them, maybe your descendants won't care about you or appreciate whatever decent or unselfish things you tried to do during your life. Would you like that?"

No Rites for a Rebel

Emma didn't reply. Strands of hair—dark, amber-black like the color of water at a mill race—tumbled over her shoulders while her fingers nervously twisted a lock of it. Her eyes glistened with tears. Seeing her distress, Bill tied a table cloth around his waist and began dropping things pretending to be a bumbling waiter. The atmosphere soon cleared and everyone was laughing.

After the last of the picnic was cleaned up, Bill helped the girls into his sleek Studebaker convertible.

"I'll take them back, Edmund. Why don't you stay for awhile and meet us at the club tonight?" There was a closeness between the two despite their disparate interests—Bill's fascination with medicine and Edmund's attraction to the military. It was an understanding that Edmund appreciated.

"Good luck," Bill said, giving a mock salute to Edmund who obviously wanted to spend the afternoon on the river searching for signs of the past. "If you see any Yankees, give the Rebel yell and take some prisoners for us."

The girls climbed into the front seat with Bill. He eased the car back carefully, dodging stumps and weaving between clumps of scrub pines and oaks toward the road that led in the direction of the Richmond highway.

Left alone, Edmund began to search for vestiges of one of the bridges. He followed the river's edge south for a couple of miles but saw nothing, and then, keeping the sunlit waters of the Chickahominy in view, he retraced his steps to the picnic site. But either the river was so high anything left of the old abutments was underwater, or the remains had long ago crumbled into the mud on the bottom of the river. All Edmund knew was that one

Near Linney's Corner, Virginia

of several bridges had been along here. He headed north, and it was rough going. The underbrush was filled with grasping honeysuckle vines and wicked briars. The day was warm and sticky, and so he sat down in a small clearing to rest.

Edmund didn't know just when he fell asleep. The last he remembered was the fragrance of wild pink roses all around him. When he waked he heard noises. But where were the sounds coming from? They seemed to be a blend of pounding hammers and the sharp crack of planks striking one another. He could also hear men's voices. Suddenly Edmund was aware of a sleeping figure lying on the ground near him—a tall well-built man. He was dressed in a Confederate uniform and beside him was a soft rakish black felt hat with a long plume tucked under its band. Was the man dead?

Leaning over him, Edmund saw that the man appeared to be breathing evenly, and he was reassured. A re-enactment must be going on nearby. But what kind of character dresses as a cavalry officer—a very important one judging from his insignia—and then lies down on the ground and falls asleep? Edmund noticed the officer's bright yellow sash and beautiful sword.

He reached out and lightly touched the man's shoulder. Eyes suddenly opened above the luxuriant beard covering most of his face, and as the blue eyes stared into his they began to twinkle. A reassuring voice said, "It's all right. Get some rest." Edmund wondered whether the man was speaking to him. Now the fellow in the general's costume was smiling, almost laughing, and saying, "Don't worry. My cavalry will get the bridge built in time, and, if not, we will all have plenty of excitement when the Yankees catch up with us." He seemed far from anxious, but in a re-enactment why should he be. Then the merry eyes closed once more.

Wait until he told Bill this. He could hear his derision. "A Confederate general lying asleep on the grass? You were dreaming!"

Edmund headed in the direction of the sounds and, looking through the briars, he could see he was approaching a clearing beside the river. Were the noises beginning to fade away a little? What would he find?

The rest of the picnic party had not ridden far in the sleek gold Studebaker convertible when they saw their road to the main highway filled with gray-clad horsemen led by a cavalry officer. He was wearing black leather boots that came up to his thigh, a hat sporting a black feather, and a brilliant yellow sash. Tall, lean, he was an impressive figure astride his mount.

"That's just how Stuart must have looked," exclaimed an awe-struck Bill, pointing to the man.

"We're in the middle of some damned re-enactment!" exclaimed Leslie, her red lips pouting again. "We'll never get home on time now."

"Those fellows really know how to ride. It's like a scene out of the past," said Bill. "What a dashing sight they are! And the blue-coated Federal cavalry waits for them up at the crest of the hill, the sun hitting their sabers. I'd like to be a re-enactor. I might think for a while that I really was my great-grandfather."

Leslie looked at him strangely. "Well, just so you weren't your great-great-uncle. You know where he was killed?"

General Stuart wore black leather boots to the thigh, a hat sporting a black feather, and a magnificent sword.

No Rites for a Rebel

"Vaguely. Wasn't it with J. E. B. Stuart?"

"That's what Edmund's always saying."

"It probably appeared pretty much as we're seeing it right now. Let's watch," urged Bill.

"What else? We can't go anywhere," Leslie replied sarcastically. "I had just as soon get caught in a funeral myself."

"You will someday. We all will," said Bill sharply. It had been months since he had been infatuated with Leslie. Now he couldn't imagine why, despite her loveliness, he had not seen her then as she really was—selfish, superficial, and more than a little callous.

Bill carefully edged the Studebaker off the road onto a low shoulder and came to a stop close to the trees. Everyone got out and stood leaning against the gleaming finish of the car watching the Confederates approach the hill where the cavalrymen waited for them. The forest hemmed the soldiers in on either side.

Bill Latané's hand touched the chrome where the sun shone upon it and almost seared the skin. He looked down quickly, jerking his hand, and as he did his eye caught a small splash of white in the carpet of leaves. While the others stared at the re-enactment, Bill reached down curiously. It was a square of cream-colored silk, somewhat decomposed, but in a corner, still visible, were the initials W. L. embroidered by hand. He studied the cloth curiously.

They were *his* initials! The material was so fine that it could probably have been drawn through the single link of gold chain that pierced each side of his grandfather's pocket-watch stem.

Recovering from his surprise he looked back at the

Near Linney's Corner, Virginia

cavalrymen and for the first time he was certain. This was a re-enactment of J. E. B. Stuart's famous ride around McClellan's army in June, 1862. A hundred years had passed since that event; it was now 1962. What was Stuart's motto? "You gallop to attack and canter if you have to retreat." I guess that was so a retreat didn't turn into a rout, he thought.

The Confederates spurred their horses and, waving their sabers, began galloping furiously toward the Union cavalrymen. Four abreast, they charged. The young officer of the lead squadron, probably a captain, thought Bill, spurred his horse and hurtled forward ahead of his men shouting, "On to them boys!"

With raised saber the officer dashed toward his Federal counterpart. Bill held his breath. The charge looked real. The Confederate, now within arms' length of his opponent, raised his saber and the blade was a silver streak in the sunlight. It slashed the air, delivering a heavy blow to the neck of the Federal captain. At the same moment the Federal officer fired two revolver shots at close range, and the Confederate slumped, then pitched off his horse. Several men leaped to the ground to pick him up.

Suddenly something struck Bill like a blow to his midriff. It was *here* that his ancestor had been killed!

His face whitened and his heart thumped. Then he felt foolish. The charge and what he was imagining to be the death of the Confederate officer were no doubt all a part of the re-enactment—albeit a very good one—of whatever had taken place years ago. The young people watched as the Confederates opened fire with carbines and shotguns, and despite the loss of the officer in the

No Rites for a Rebel

first charge it was obvious the Confederates would be victorious.

With a start they were brought back to the present by the rumble and roar of truck motors as a long convoy from one of Virginia's military bases approached, not a mile away, and headed toward them up the hill. The three youths turned and stared back down the road in dismay, their trip back to Richmond delayed even more. Bill realized with distaste that the handkerchief he had picked up from the ground was damp—no, wet. To his astonishment his fingers were stained blood red! "Damn!" he exclaimed softly.

The others had begun to count aloud, competing in trying to estimate the number of military vehicles. But the long line stretched off in the distance as far as they could see. When they turned dispiritedly back to the re-enactment, the Civil War soldiers were nowhere to be seen. Perhaps they were beyond the crest of the hill or had detoured through the woods and cross country rather than be delayed by such a large convoy. In any case, they were gone.

Rays of sunlight splayed across the crest of the hill and seemed to rest upon a caravan of camouflaged vehicles as the mechanized roar of the army of the twentieth century rumbling past pushed back into memory the terrified whinnies of wounded horses and wild Rebel yells.

"My God!" Leslie screamed. "What's wrong with your hand, Bill?" To his astonishment he saw that the handkerchief he had picked up was now dripping blood.

"You look like you're bleeding to death! What *did* you do to yourself?"

He bound the handkerchief awkwardly around a fin-

Near Linney's Corner, Virginia

ger, inventing an excuse quickly. "Pierced my finger on a thorn—nothing more." Then he worried for fear that concern might make her ask to examine his finger or help him staunch the blood, but he should have known Leslie better.

Bill was amazed at how wet the handkerchief had become. Since it was not his own, whose blood was it?

He thought of wounds that bled mysteriously on religious statues, eyes of graven images that shed tears. Strange, utterly miraculous stories passed through his mind, and when he looked at his stained hand, his stomach felt queasy. Could it somehow be the blood of his dead Confederate ancestor?

Stepping back from the road to avoid the heat and exhaust fumes that accompanied the convoy, he leaned against a pine and felt the rough bark through his shirt. He squinched his intelligent gray eyes to narrow slits in the bright sunlight as, mesmerized by the blur of camouflage colors, he tried to collect himself and watch the green, ocher, and tan splotched vehicles pass. But Bill Latané was not really thinking about the convoy. Words of a century-old poem had begun to echo through his mind—a poem he had commited to memory. Its sentiments—sad, romantic, typical of the era—were an incongruous accompaniment to men shouting wisecracks to each other from the rolling, rattling, rumbling, thundering, steady line of military vehicles a few yards away.

The words of the poem were

No man of God might say the burial rite
Above the "rebel"—thus declared the foe
But woman's voice, in accents soft and low,

No Rites for a Rebel

Trembling with pity, touched with pathos, read
Over his hallowed dust the ritual for the dead.

It was from the famous elegy written about his great-great-uncle Captain William Latané, the only man J. E. B. Stuart had lost during his daring reconnaissance ride around McClellan. After the crossing of the Chicka-hominy and on the way to Linney's Corner, Latané made a bold charge ahead of his men and had been struck by two pistol shots. Pitching from his horse, he was dead when he hit the ground.

Twenty-nine-year-old Latané, a practicing physician before the war, died on June 13. His brother and fellow officers picked up his body and hurriedly made arrange-ments with a Virginia family to give it a proper burial nearby. Then they rejoined Stuart. Later it was learned that the women had to say the funeral rite over the grave themselves. This was enemy country and no clergyman could be found who would hold a burial service for a Confederate.

The date of June 13 kept surfacing in Bill's mind. Today was also June 13, and hadn't he been often told by his grandmother that young William was an ancestor of his? He looked again at the initials—"W. L."—as he was to look at them many times during the years ahead. And he wondered if the man he had seen fall from his horse atop the hill had somehow sensed his presence, had in some mysterious way actually used his own blood to send a message of love and concern into the future.

Only one other person believed Bill's story after-ward—another descendant of Stuart's handpicked cav-alry that June, 1862. It was Edmund. Perhaps because

Near Linney's Corner, Virginia

Edmund had his own strange experience, or as he often called it later, a dream.

He had seen a tall man with laughing eyes asleep on the grass in the glen and believed he had glimpsed Stuart resting there as the general confidently waited for a miracle—waited for his cavalrymen to build a bridge across the river in two hours—build it swiftly, build it before he and all his men were trapped between pursuing Federal troops and the turbulent, swiftly flowing waters of the rain-swollen Chickahominy.

Edmund knew the story of the challenge Stuart had faced. Federal troops were beginning to realize that a body of Confederate cavalrymen was in their midst. They were in pursuit. When the Confederates reached the place where they usually forded the river, they found that several days of rain had made it impassable. They cut trees and desperately tumbled them into the river, but the trees were too short.

Stuart ordered his expert horsemen, many of them aristocrats and gentlemen farmers, to build a bridge immediately. According to his report of the crisis, these inexperienced but highly motivated bridge builders managed to finish not a moment too soon! His cavalry crossed the bridge and had just reluctantly thrown pine torches upon it to set it afire when pursuing Union cavalry galloped out of the woods. As the Federal troops watched in frustration, the crude bridge blazed fiercely, sending up noisy, spluttering bursts of sparks and a wall of flame twenty-five feet high. The Confederates safely cantered on their way toward Richmond.

No Rites for a Rebel

But what of the picnickers?

Edmund decided afterward to investigate the activities of Civil War groups that day. The investigation revealed that a re-enactment had been planned for that day but was canceled after a check revealed the probable presence of a military convoy in the area.

Bill later searched his own body for any wound or scratch that might have shed blood and found none. He had the handkerchief, bearing what was once more only a reddish brown stain, analyzed to be certain that it could not possibly be his blood. It was not. The handkerchief, authenticated by a museum curator as a Civil War relic, is now a valued family keepsake.

Did the blood of a man who had died a century before actually liquify for a matter of minutes? Bill Latané will never know.

Richmond—

    As the Davis government evacuated Richmond on the night of April 2, 1865, fire raged out of control while pillagers and drunken mobs roamed the streets looting and burning. On the morning of April 3, Federal troops got the fire under control and restored order. A Richmond woman who saw the Confederate flag that fluttered above the Capitol come down said, "We covered our faces and cried aloud."

ooo

RICHMOND'S UNION HEROINE

Richmond, Virginia

"Family diaries can reveal strange stories, and my mother's is certainly one of them," said the Richmond matron as our tour bus drove along Grace Street. A native of the city taking a "busman's holiday," she pointed out her home.

"I have read my mother's diary so often I think I know every word. She wrote that as a child she often saw the 'infamous' Elizabeth Van Lew surrounded by her many cats, the only beings, it seemed, that would communicate with her.

"By my mother's account:

    Miss Van Lew was a small, frail, solitary figure in a black dress who sometimes sat in the shade on the steps of the great house beside the tall white columns. She was old by then. Little boys taunted her when they saw her on the street and called her "Crazy Bett." Little girls were terrified of her.

Richmond's Union Heroine

Our houses here on East Grace Street were not far apart. At night, I would sometimes walk to the end of this street and stand inside the metal cable that was there then, fascinated by the lights forming a huge glittering multicolored quilt of the city below.

One night I heard a stick break as it might under foot. Then a faint rustle. "Crazy Bett" with her hooded, piercing eyes stood beside me. I know I jumped, but I was proud of myself because I didn't run.

"You're the Adams girl, aren't you?" she said abruptly, and I answered, "Yes."

"I thought I recognized you from the back by that long, lank hair of yours."

Then she began talking about how well you could see the city from here and pointed out the Tredegar Iron Works. When the Union troops occupied Richmond it was the only building left standing after the fire.

I was nervous as could be, because no one talked with Miss Van Lew, and as soon as I could I excused myself saying, "I've got to get home so my mama won't worry."

"Stay . . . please stay a while and talk with me," she pleaded, and I just shook my head and scampered away. Mother said Miss Van Lew wouldn't hurt me but not to tell grandmother that I had been talking with her.

"Mother explained, "No one ever goes to visit her, and she's lonely since she came back from Washington. People despise her since the war."

"What did she do?" I asked.

Richmond, Virginia

"She helped the enemy."

"But that's been a long time ago."

"Folks have long memories. Some lost sons, fathers, husbands. In their hearts I'm sure they said, this woman whom we befriended helped kill our loved ones. She gave information to the Yankees. Because of that they hate her."

"Why do they call her 'Crazy Bett'?"

"Some say she put on silly ways when she made trips to Libby Prison to visit Federal officers, so the prison officials would think her harmless and let her carry in gifts of food. But I don't think she was crazy at all. Her name is Elizabeth Van Lew, and I'll tell you more about her someday," said mother, turning her head toward the hall. There was the tapping sound of grandmother's cane.

"Viper in our bosom! That's what Elizabeth Van Lew was," said my grandmother.

"Why Gran, what did she do?"

"She betrayed her friends, people who had entertained her in their homes and accepted her as one of them, men who had traded with her father and helped make him rich. She knew the husbands of her *friends*"—Gran used the word with bitter sarcasm— "could die because of her treachery." Gran's faded blue eyes flashed with an awesome fire. "What do you think of a woman like that?"

Mother told me more, a little at a time, and I decided to write it down. I had always wanted to be a writer, and my father said Miss Elizabeth was quite a character, that her life would probably make a good

story. A sad story, in my opinion. It was years later
before I took my childish scrawlings and began to
gather more material—some from Official Records of
the Union and Confederate Armies, some from news-
papers, some from people who knew her and also
from her own diary that was found buried in the yard
at her house.

I found out that as a girl Miss Van Lew was educated in Philadelphia where her father had been
mayor before the family moved to Richmond. Here
his hardware business prospered.

There were balls and receptions in the Van Lew
house, famous guests such as Chief Justice Marshall,
the Lees, the Adamses, Fredrika Bremer the Swedish
novelist, and Edgar Allan Poe. Jenny Lind, at the
height of her career, sang in the Van Lews' elegant
parlor. They entertained often and had many friends.

Long before the Civil War Miss Van Lew's anti-
slavery views were well known, and everyone assumed she had picked them up while she was at
school in Philadelphia. Miss Van Lew showed Fredrika Bremer a tobacco factory where, as Miss
Bremer later wrote, upon observing the working conditions, "the hard lot and sad faces of the slave workers, the good Miss Van L. could not refrain from
weeping." As the 1850s passed, the family freed their
house servants and sent a young black girl named
Mary Elizabeth Bowser north for an education.

By the opening of the Civil War Miss Van Lew was
a spinster of forty-two. She was a small woman, reso-
lute and with a quick intellect. When other Rich-

Richmond, Virginia

mond women gathered to sew clothing and knit for Confederate soldiers, Miss Van Lew was not among them.

Meanwhile, from the capital of the Confederacy, she wrote dispatches to the Union—information about Southern troops, their numbers and their movements. She sent the messages through the lines by special courier. Bull Run was fought and wounded Southern soldiers and Northern prisoners began streaming into the city. Miss Van Lew, because of her social position, received written permission from Confederate general Winder to "visit the prisoners and to send them books, luxuries, delicacies and whatever you may wish."

The commanding officer at Libby Prison was Lieutenant Todd, the Confederate brother of Mrs. Mary Todd Lincoln. With gifts of buttermilk and gingerbread Miss Van Lew won his good will. She also visited two other prisons in the area. But Libby was her special care, and the building was at the base of Church Hill—almost beneath her very door. From the time she first gained access to the men through Lieutenant Todd, her dispatches to the Federal commanders about Southern military movements increased a hundredfold in value. Her hospital and prison charities were, according to a postwar *Harper's Monthly* article about her, another source of information—"a cloak to cover her real mission. Miss Van Lew was a spy."

The writer of the *Harper's* story says the prisoners on Belle Isle and in Libby furnished her with accurate estimations of the strength of passing troops and

Richmond's Union Heroine

information about supply trains. They shrewdly conjectured destinations by the roads on which the Confederates left town, from the talk of surgeons who treated Rebel soldiers, or by overhearing guards. This is certainly possible with luck, but the accuracy of information conveyed by prisoners who did not know the city or where most of the roads led and whose informants were most often passing along gossip is debatable. Many errors were made in ascertaining the number of the enemy by Federal generals who actually had scouts in the field. It would seem Miss Van Lew had other sources considerably more reliable—perhaps placed in the household of Jefferson Davis himself.

In an effort to pass along information, the prisoners slipped little notes with hidden meanings. Questions and answers were concealed in baskets of food or in books with words or a page number lightly underlined.

Occasionally a prison guard would become suspicious, and now and then Miss Van Lew's permit to visit the prison was revoked, but she would go to General Winder. Believing her motives sincere, as the Bible admonished, this good Christian gentleman would overrule the prohibition of a suspicious lower-level prison official. And so by flattery, social position, and her feigned idiosyncracies, Miss Van Lew succeeded most of the time in hoodwinking the authorities.

The war dragged on, and the first years of victory and glory turned into days and nights when the streets echoed with the ceaseless roll of wagon wheels

Richmond, Virginia

bearing Richmond's dead and wounded sons home. Since many of the farms near Richmond that provided food for the city had been devastated by battles, the winter of 1862–63 was one of hardship. Food was hoarded and many were in serious want. One morning a crowd of four to five hundred gathered in Capitol Square, and a woman taking a walk before breakfast asked a young girl whether there was a celebration. "There is," she replied. "We celebrate our right to life. We are starving. . . . We are going to the bakeries and each of us will take a loaf of bread." The crowd began to move down 9th Street and it finally took President Jefferson Davis himself to disperse them. Both the well-off and the poor were affected by the food shortage.

In the last months of the war, Miss Van Lew's ridiculous mannerisms—humming, vacant smiles, mincing steps with a skip now and then as she made her way down 10th Street on her way to Libby Prison— probably helped her gain entrance. To the guards she was only "Crazy Bett," and they paid her little heed. But the people of Richmond by now suspected that she had betrayed her neighbors and the South.

If any of the Federal officers in Libby were able to escape, she hid them in a secret chamber of her columned house on East Grace Street. Long years after the war—after Miss Van Lew's death—her niece visited the old house and the secret room. It had been more than forty years since her fingers went over the panelled walls and touched the hidden spring. She told of one other time when she had stealthily followed Aunt Betty up through the dark hall and into

Richmond's Union Heroine

an unused room to see where she was carrying a plate of food at night. As she peered fearfully into the attic from the head of the stairs and saw the shadows and the ghostly shapes of the old furniture, she saw her aunt standing before a black hole in the wall with a candle in her upraised hand. In its yellow glow the child saw the face of a soldier—shaggy-haired and bearded.

In the library there was yet another secret hiding place behind one of the ornamental lions on either side of the fireplace. The statue was loose and could be raised slightly to expose a shallow cavity beneath it. Here Miss Van Lew would slip messages written in code, and later an old black servant, alone in the room dusting, would remove it and plod down the road to a nearby farm. The servant would bear tidings such as news of the departure from the city of General Longstreet's corps to rejoin Lee and the location of the road north on which Longstreet might be intercepted and attacked.

Miss Van Lew continued to dispatch whatever news she could to jeopardize the Confederates. Of the many dispatches she sent, however, only one survived. She must have destroyed the others returned to her later by the War Department. The surviving message concerned the planned removal of prisoners from Libby Prison to Georgia, for the need to defend Richmond was desperate. The large number of Federal prisoners constituted a danger to the city.

On the basis of Miss Van Lew's message that this move was in the offing, Federal generals decided upon the Kilpatrick-Dahlgren Raid to try to rescue Federal

Richmond, Virginia

prisoners. The raid failed, although it penetrated within five miles of Richmond. Like Confederate general John Bell Hood, who with an amputated leg rode to fight at Franklin, Tennessee, Colonel Dahlgren, an artificial limb taking the place of the leg he lost a few months before, led a handful of exhausted men into King and Queen County. There the little band rode into an ambush, and Colonel Dahlgren was shot dead. A coffin was made, and the Confederates buried him at the fork of the two roads where he was killed. Since anger in the city ran high about the attempt to storm the prison, a few days later the body was disinterred, brought to Richmond, and buried in a safer place.

Perhaps Miss Van Lew's most dramatic exploit was her purchase of the metal casket and the engineering of the theft of the body. It was stolen at midnight, removed from its wooden casket and carried at great risk to the farm of a German family where it was reburied. When Admiral Dahlgren requested the body of his son from the Confederacy, the Confederate government made every effort to comply—an action that came as a great surprise to the Richmond Union sympathizers who believed the Confederates to be too bitter toward Dahlgren to honor the request. But when the Confederates sought to comply, they were bewildered to discover that the body had disappeared. The location of the remains was not revealed until after the war, when the son's body was returned to his father.

Close upon the heels of the Dahlgren incident came the spring campaign and as Elizabeth Van Lew was gratified to write in her diary, "the army (Federal)

Richmond's Union Heroine

has closed around Richmond, and I was able to communicate with General Butler (unflatteringly termed "Beast" Butler by Southerners!) and General Grant, but not so well and persistently with General Butler for there was too much danger in the system.

"With General Grant, through his Chief of Secret Service, General George H. Sharpe, I was more fortunate," wrote Miss Van Lew.

She was so fortunate that flowers picked for him in her garden one day would grace General Grant's breakfast table the next morning. One can imagine the grizzled general's pleasure.

Miss Van Lew's contacts extended even into the home of the president of the Confederacy. She sent Mary Elizabeth Bowser, the free black girl who had been educated in the North, to apply for the job of a domestic in the home of Jefferson Davis. In the midst of the comings and goings of generals, military conferences, and important messages, the girl had the freedom of the house and often waited on family and guests at the table. It is ironic to speculate whether Mary Elizabeth Bowser may even have overheard General Robert E. Lee futilely implore President Davis to issue a proclamation to free the slaves in the South. But of more immediate importance to the Army of the Potomac were the plans of Confederate generals that this woman heard almost daily.

One spring evening, Mrs. Mary Boykin Chestnut, writer of a famous diary of the period, went by the Davis house to pay a call. It was the family dinner hour, and as she waited outside she listened to a general "tell us how things stood. He said that General

Richmond, Virginia

Stoneman's cavalry raid was moving on Richmond, and there were no reserves to check them."

Mrs. Davis came out shortly, and as the two women talked, Mrs. Chestnut commented on "how dreadful it is that the enemy is within 40 miles from us—only 40!"

"Who told you that tale?" asked Varina Davis. "They are within three miles of Richmond!"

On January 19, 1865, during a large reception, an attempt was made to burn down the Davis home. A fire was kindled in a woodpile in the basement but a servant noticed the smoke and sounded the alarm barely in time to save the house and guests. The young Davis children were frightened but safe. That same night the house was robbed and two servants were found missing. Elizabeth Bowser was one of them, and Miss Van Lew was later known to be involved.

As suspicion turned to fury toward Elizabeth Van Lew she received threats to drive her away. In truth, it would have been better for Richmond if they had shipped her off to some Northern city. But the respect the family once enjoyed, highly placed friends still reluctant to believe Elizabeth Van Lew was a spy, and traditional Southern gallantry toward women restrained any violence toward her.

Winter was hardly over when Lee's veterans—gaunt, ragged, and immeasurably heroic—resumed the now hopeless struggle. The desperate Confederacy was ransacking the South to replace horses for its fighting men. Miss Van Lew rolled up her Oriental rugs and hid her horse in the study of her home while

Richmond's Union Heroine

she looked forward to the last days of the city. As Federal troops approached and members of the Confederate government left by train, mobs rioted in the streets and buildings were set afire. She had a dramatic view of the burning city from the bluff at the end of East Grace Street, half a block from her home.

Richmond had fallen.

Fifteen days after his inauguration President Grant appointed Miss Van Lew postmaster of Richmond, complimenting her as his finest spy. Had she demanded the office in payment for her services? In any event, disregarding the tight-lipped contempt of the people of Richmond, she served as postmaster in the city for eight years. After her removal from office, poverty overtook her, and the comment of Southerners was, "The South would not have forsaken her the way the North has done, had she espoused the Southern cause."

She was finally reduced to writing to Northern friends for help, and the family and relatives of Colonel Paul Revere, whom she had aided in Libby Prison, gave her an ample annuity for her remaining years.

But there was much that money would never buy.

"I live—have lived for years—as entirely distinct from the citizens, as if I were plague-stricken," she wrote. "Rarely, very rarely, is our door-bell ever rung by any but a pauper, or those desiring my service. September 1875, my mother was taken from me by death. *We did not have enough friends to be pall-bearers.*"

Dressed in many frills, Miss Van Lew could be seen

Richmond, Virginia

almost every night walking alone on Grace Street. When darkness fell, the front door would open. Down the front walk of her dilapidated house she would come with her cane. She would pause to fumble with the latch of the gate and then the diminutive black-clad figure would make her way slowly along the street until she reached the bluff to stand looking out over the city. She was bitter and lonely. It is no wonder she was glad to talk to the child who liked to come there, too.

I was standing alone one April night at the end of East Grace Street looking out over the city and thinking how beautiful it was. It was hot for this time of year, and I hadn't worn a coat over my short-sleeved dress. Suddenly something brushed my bare arm, and I started. I turned my head and there stood Miss Elizabeth Van Lew. Her gray hair, fluffy around her forehead, and the tiny beribboned hat she always wore perched on her head, even at night, must have touched me.

"It's pretty, isn't it?" I said. We never talked about the war, and I felt sorry for her.

"Yes," she replied, and then she went on, "I guess they will be sending someone by to see me about my taxes soon."

I knew what she meant. Since women could not vote she never paid her taxes and had said many times, as she did tonight, "It's taxation without representation, you know." And I nodded.

That was the last time I saw her—at least alive. Miss Van Lew died in 1900. When she went to a lonely grave in Shockoe Cemetery her only tribute came from Boston. Two years later the city sent a slab of gray stone with a brown tablet on it and an inscription which reads in part: "She risked everything that is dear to man—friends, fortune, comfort, health, life itself, all for the one absorbing desire of her heart, that slavery be abolished and the Union preserved."

Perhaps the reason she has appeared to me since is because even though I was a child, I was one of the few people who was nice to her. She never frightened me. And as long as my home is here on Church Hill, it seems possible to me that I may again see the apparition of Elizabeth Van Lew.

The last occasion was during World War II, and I was more than normally worried about my son. As I walked to my usual place of meditation, I thought I heard faint steps in the dry leaves behind me, but each time I looked back no one was there. Finally, I reached the rail that encircles the end of the street to keep one from driving off the bluff.

When I was in turmoil, it was a place to be alone and think. On rare occasions, I thought I sensed Miss Van Lew's presence, particularly when a cat—I think she owned forty!—would wander up as it did that night to rub against my legs. The year was 1943, and I recall standing out there trying to keep from wringing my hands with worry over my son.

Then I suddenly realized that I was almost surrounded by cats! I tried to ignore them. Suddenly I felt a gentle pat upon my shoulder, heard the soft rustle of taffeta. When I turned, I saw a small figure in black wearing an old-fashioned high white collar.

Richmond, Virginia

She seemed to be holding out her hands toward me, and before I could speak, a woman's voice said in crisp, urgent tones, "We must get these flowers through the lines at once. They're for General Grant's breakfast table in the morning."

When I recovered from my shock, she was gone, taking every cat with her but one. There was the final soft flick of a silky tail upon my bare leg, and then the last cat vanished."

ooo

"This story was told to me by my mother who died in the 1960s," said a Richmond tour guide in June, 1991.

Charleston—
On the night of February 17, 1865, Confederate troops marched quietly from a courageous city that had been exhorted to fight to the last. Trains left every few minutes with citizens and their valuables, commissary supplies rolled out, hospitals moved patients by wagon to the interior. The evacuation was smooth, for it had been anticipated. Besieged for so long, this strategic Southern port was about to fall. As a final act of defiance a new Confederate flag had been raised that morning, replacing the tattered garrison flag at Fort Sumter. On February 18, 1865, it was lowered by Union troops and the Stars and Stripes was hoisted forevermore at Sumter. The troops entering that day were the first Federals to set foot in Charleston since 1861.

○○○

THE SLAVE AND THE STRAW HAT

Charleston, South Carolina

Sometimes a man's whole life may hang upon a trivial thing, and that was the way it was for me.

My wife, Maggie, and I had been aiming, ever since our marriage, to buy our freedom from Mr. Henry McKee, and he had agreed to it. I was ridin' high that spring day in 1862 with my first week's pay from the Confederate steamer in my pocket. The captain of *The Planter* had paid me generously. At this rate I would be able to buy Maggie's freedom and mine, too, in a year—the Lord willing.

Lytch, the plantation overseer, was waiting on the dock. I had always turned over to him the paltry pay I earned working for various tradesmen. Then he paid me. Today, when I handed him my money, I thought I would burst with pride while I stood waiting for him to give me back some bills. He handed me one. I guess he saw the look on my face 'cause he said, "Robert Smalls, Mr. Henry went and let you get married 'gainst my better judgment. Now I've got both you and your wife to keep up." He put some of the bills in his jacket for Mr. Henry and stuffed the rest in his own britches pocket.

"But, I'm trying to save to buy our freedom. Mr. Henry knows that's what I'm workin' for," I said desperately.

"Don't get impudent, nigger!" he said, his eyes blazing. Then he added, "Wal, mebbe that's somethin' we could talk about—in a year or two." He wheeled to go, then turned, his yellowed teeth showing in an ugly smile. "I'll be back here waitin' next week. And you better give me all your pay, you black rascal."

Maggie wasn't in the cabin when I got home. She worked for Old Missus up at the big house, and if I got home first, I'd take the broom and sweep the sand clean where the chickens had messed up the yard, then sit on the porch to wait for her. But today I just went in and lay across the bed. I felt po'ly—mighty po'ly. Never had reckoned on Old Lytch keepin' back that much . . . both from me and the master. Mr. Henry would sure be angry if he knew.

"Robert, Robert! What you doin' lyin' up here in the dark," I heard Maggie say. She came in and sat down close to me on the bed.

"You sick?" I was sick, all right, but not sick the way she meant.

"Robert, turn over and look at me." I did and when I saw her so frail and pretty starin' down at me, her eyes big with worry, I began to kind of catch my breath. My shoulders heaved, but my eyes stayed dry.

The Slave and the Straw Hat

"Robert! What's wrong?"

"Old Lytch. He'll never let me get my freedom."

"But you can buy it—Mr. Henry said so."

"Not on what Lytch gives me out of my pay, Maggie." I showed her the bill still clutched in my hand.

"I don't believe it!" We held each other tight.

"Robert, you got to tell Mr. Henry what Lytch's doin'. He's stealing from you both. Mr. Henry knows him. He'll believe you."

"I been thinkin' about that. But you know what would happen sometime when the master is away? You remember how Lytch had Big Buck flogged?"

"It almost killed him," Maggie grimaced. "He never could see out of one eye where the whip curled around and hit the side of his face."

"Yes and he'd get me, too, Maggie . . . someday when Mr. Henry wan't here to stop him." She was silent.

Late that night Maggie brought up the subject of freedom again. "Isn't there anything we could do?" She moved within the circle of my arms as we lay in bed.

"It's more important than ever now."

"What do you mean, *now?*"

"Since we're going to have a baby."

"God Almighty! That's good news, Maggie!" I blurted the words out, but then I thought again. "Lordy, I don't know when Lytch will give me enough of my pay to buy three people."

"I wish there was some way we could leave before the baby comes."

"Before the baby comes? How? That's crazy, honey."

Charleston, South Carolina

ooo

I had started working on the big steamer in early January, and each week that passed, I knew more about what I was doin'. Sometimes I took the wheel for Captain Relyea. When he was teaching me how to read the charts, the captain had me take *The Planter* up some of the small streams. Our ship had an advantage because she only drew a little over three feet of water, and she could maneuver like a fish through those shallow coastal creeks.

One evening we had a little excitement. Out past Fort Sumter and not far from Morris Island the Federal blockaders waited, hungry as sharks. As we steamed back into port, a Federal blockader followed in our wake.

"We got the fastest vessel in the harbor of Charleston," bragged Captain Relyea to me, his old straw hat perched on his head at its usual rakish angle. We were leaving the blockader farther and farther behind, and watching it from the stern, we grinned at each other proudly.

"Give the fort the signal, Robert," he shouted to me. "We don't want Sumter's guns to sink us by mistake. A broadside would smash us to matchsticks."

I blew the correct signal with the ship's whistle, and we passed the Confederate sentry. Our ship was a three-hundred-ton twin-engine woodburner and her berth was at Southern Wharf, barely a hundred yards from the Confederate general's headquarters. This area around the wharf swarmed with our sentries.

After the captain's and my adventure with the blockader, I spent the next day with the men swabbing decks

The Slave and the Straw Hat

and polishing brass. Captain Relyea was ashore. Playfully one of the other slaves who was a deckhand snatched Relyea's battered straw hat from its usual place in the pilot house and clapped it on my head. "If you don't look jus' like the Cap'n himself!" said Bennie.

"What's our orders, Cap'n?" he asked, and the other deckhands doubled up with laughter. I had just been promoted to first-class pilot and didn't like all this clowning. Only yesterday Captain Relyea had pointed me out to Mr. Adger Smythe, *The Planter*'s owner, saying, "This is Robert Small. He's goin' to make a name for himself as a navigator."

But despite my pleasure over how much I was learning on *The Planter,* I was becoming more and more discouraged. I'd never have enough money to buy Maggie's freedom and my own, much less our baby's. Mr. Henry had promised, and he was a decent man. He hadn't meant for that devil Lytch to cheat me. One afternoon I saw Mr. Henry near the stable and was goin' to tell him how Lytch was stealing from us both when the overseer himself suddenly appeared. I walked on to my cabin, like I hadn't seen Mr. Henry. If I had begun to tell him, Lytch would have heard me. It was a close call.

When I reached the cabin, Maggie was sitting in a chair with a blanket over her knees. "The midwife say I need to stay off my feet, Robert, or I may lose this baby."

"How can you do that without telling the Missus why? When is your time?"

"Three or four months—if I don't lose it."

"Mr. Henry's wife is a good woman, and she knows how Lytch is. First thing she'd do would be to let him know why you were not workin'."

Charleston, South Carolina

We ate in silence—a bowl of field peas, some collard greens and corn pone. I was thinking as hard as I could, and Maggie was too discouraged to talk. Soon as I finished eating I stood up.

"I'm going over to Bennie's tonight, Maggie."

"You're not plannin' on shootin' dice are you? Bennie's a great one to gamble."

"No."

"Isn't that where some of the deckhands get together . . . the one's who're always complaining?"

"There's that kind in any group, Maggie."

"Yes, but they get together at Bennie's. If Lytch finds out . . ."

"He's not going to. I got my reasons, Maggie," and with that I closed the cabin door behind me.

When I went in the first thing someone said to me was, "Well, what's this white chicken doin' here with all us black ones?" Everybody ha, ha'ed, and I smiled, tryin' to remember these were the same fellows I joked with every day on the steamer. Only one there any different was me.

"You're not lookin' at a white chicken tonight," I says, and that's how the talk began. I didn't leave out of there until after midnight, and when I got home Maggie was awake and worryin'.

"We done run out of time, Maggie," I said.

And I began explaining our plan to her. At first she was scared to death. Then that fiery spirit I always admired in her began to come back, and she was with me all the way. We had decided to move fast. Something could change and make it impossible. At any time *The Planter* might be sent out on a voyage. All that next week

The Slave and the Straw Hat

I lived in dread that somebody would give us away—that Old Lytch would hear. I was sure every loud knock on our door was his big hand.

On the night of May 12, seven of us—one at a time—strolled past the sentry actin' just as calm and casual as could be. We met aboard *The Planter.* Now came the hardest part. Waiting. We were all quiet until about three o'clock in the morning when I finally gave the order to fire up. Smoke from the ship's stack began to drift toward the city, and all I could do was worry—worry that people in Charleston might smell it and think someone's house was afire. They'd sound an alarm. It seemed like the next thirty minutes would never pass but they finally did, and when 3:30 A.M. came we cast off the lines from the wharf.

As the dark shape of *The Planter* edged away from the pilings, I saw a sentry. My heart began thumping. He must have thought we were on routine business because he didn't challenge us, and on we went. Looming up ahead in the dark was the steamer *Etowah,* and just like we planned, we slid gently along side her. The ship was deserted—except for Maggie and our crew's wives and children who were hidden on it. I waited for one of the little 'uns to start cryin', but they didn't. The babies slept right through it, and everyone boarded quietly and went below. So far a miracle. But the hardest part lay ahead. I was skittish as a runaway slave who thinks the "pateroler" has tracked him down and there come the footsteps right behind him.

Turning the wheel, I steered *The Planter* east toward the sea. It was all I could do to resist giving her every

Charleston, South Carolina

bit of power she had, but I knew better. I had to go slow and not arouse suspicion. If I ran her fast past Fort Sumter in the dark, we'd be challenged for sure.

Maggie sat behind me, and now and then she'd say something encouraging. Brave as can be she was, despite her condition. I kept edging *The Planter* along, not wanting to pull even with the fort until it was light enough for them to see us. We'd have to pass it now in about five minutes, and my chest was so tight I could hardly breathe. A burst from one of their guns was all it would take to sink us, and I thought of Maggie and the baby I would never see. Another thing. What if my whistle didn't sound *just right* to the fort sentry? They would fire sure 'nuf. At 4:15 it was time to put on some steam and pass Sumter.

I reached for Captain Relyea's old hat and put it on my head. Standing in plain view I turned so the sentinel at the fort would only see the profile of that hat and not my color. My hands on the wheel were slippery, they were so wet with sweat. Bennie stood near me. He said he saw the sentry on the parapet take a few steps and speak to another man who was walking up beside him. I knew he was reporting our guard boat going out. The other man was the officer of the day.

"They must be suspicious," I said in a voice so hoarse it didn't sound like my own.

"Blow the whistle, Cap'n. Hurry!" Bennie whispered urgently.

This was the moment when we would either make it or be on our way to the bottom of the harbor, but I couldn't seem to move.

The Slave and the Straw Hat

"Blow it!" snapped Bennie. My hands still hadn't left the wheel.

"If you don't, I'll do it myself!"

That snapped me into action. I reached over and blew the steamer's whistle. Boats occasionally left at this hour, and it must have sounded like the right signal because the officer of the day walked away. No one at the fort took any further notice of us. Lord, I was tremblin'.

We were still alive but we had something else just as dangerous—maybe even more so—to do next. We could get ourselves blown to bits, and I wasn't sure the crew knew what a close call this next move would be. Normally I'd go out beyond the fort and then turn and head slowly to the Morris Island landing. This time—just before I reached the point to turn—I shouted, "Fire the boiler and give her every bit of steam she has, boys!" I was prayin' while *The Planter* headed straight for the Federal blockaders.

Looking through the binoculars I saw figures runnin' on the decks of the Federal gun boats. Men were gettin' ready to fire, and I expected the impact of their shells to blast us out of the water any second. But Bennie was thinking fast. While we sped toward the Yankee ships he was hauling *The Planter*'s Confederate flag down and hoisting a white sheet. One of the blockaders hadn't seen the white square sliding up that rope and, to my horror, I saw they were going to fire. "Duck, men!" I shouted and waited. At the last possible moment the Yankees noticed our white flag, and I surrendered my vessel along with its guns, a 32-pounder and a 24-pounder howitzer.

The next thing we knew a bunch of grinning fellows in blue coats were clambering over the side of *The Planter*.

Charleston, South Carolina

From that moment on everything in my life changed. In the first place I was free! So was Maggie, and best of all, so was our new baby boy. I was a slave only a few months before, but the North made me a hero, and the navy soon promoted me to captain of *The Planter*.

Looking back, I can see this all began by chance. The whole idea to steal General Rosewell S. Ripley's District Confederate Army Commander's dispatch boat started with that crazy stunt of Bennie's. Gradually it took shape in my mind sometime after he took Captain Relyea's old straw hat, jammed it on my head, and the men called me "Cap'n."

I'll always believe that straw hat started me on the road to freedom!

ooo

After the war was over Robert Smalls served as a member of the South Carolina House of Representatives and Senate, and afterward he was elected to Congress. The last years of his life were spent at Beaufort, South Carolina, where he was respected by both races.

At daybreak on the morning of March 13, 1862, Federal gun-boats commenced a bombardment of the shore at Slocum's Creek about twelve miles below New Bern by water in preparation for the landing of troops. Lacking the numbers and artillery to hold New Bern, the North Carolina troops retreated inland to Kinston, but the loss of New Bern, nearby Morehead City, and the smaller ports of North Carolina's Outer Bank was a serious blow. Troops were rushed into the state from Virginia.

OOO

THE SPY OF MOREHEAD CITY

Outer Banks of North Carolina

There was a macabre quality about the scene, as if the curtain had risen on some infernal tableau. Fog from the marsh billowed about the figures like smoke, and the light of a lantern added to the eerie effect, tinging the mist an ugly, sulphurous yellow.

Each man grappled to gain an advantage over the other. The one in jacket and seaman's trousers was short and stocky, while his adversary was tall and attired in a flowing cloak. A sharp cry of pain came from the seaman as he reeled from a blow to the mid-section. Mist closed in to conceal the pair, parted again, and in that instant when the fog lifted the cloaked figure raised his arm high. Down came the blade of a knife like a shining silver streak.

It was March 10, 1862, the second year of the War Between the States. Unaware of the bloodshed ahead, the dunes and marshlands of the Outer Banks lay in their hushed windswept isolation as they had for centuries.

At Crab Point in Morehead City, twenty-two-year-old Emeline Pigott brought supper to the Confederate soldier hiding in her family's storeroom. As she left him she heard a knock at the front door.

It was Mr. Edwin Forsyth, a wizened little man with a tanned face and sharp bright blue eyes, a frequent visitor.

"Come in. I'll call my father," said Emeline Pigott. Waiting for her father's arrival, she cringed at the sound of a faint cough from the direction of the soldier's hiding place. Had their visitor heard? With her back to him she quickly feigned a cough herself. Forsyth had always been a good friend but one couldn't be too careful. Emeline did not breathe easy until she heard her father close the front door behind his caller.

A stroll would slow her rapidly beating heart. She slipped quickly outside into the darkness and mist. Her father would try to discourage her going alone at night, if he knew about it, but she would not be long. Wearing a dark coat with a fitted bodice and full skirt and covering her hair with a white scarf to protect it from the misting rain, Emeline Pigott hurried along the empty road.

Reaching the corner of Evans and Arendell, her pace slowed. Before her lay the backwater of the Newport River, and as she made her way along the narrow winding path, she heard the faint night sounds from the water. Her tension gradually ebbed.

Stopping for a minute to retie the slipping head-scarf,

The Spy of Morehead City

she thought she heard a muffled sigh, but she dismissed the sound. It was unlikely that anyone would be out here at this hour. How foolish such thoughts were! Then, in one chilling moment, a hand shot swiftly across her mouth, and a strong arm encircled her waist.

"Don't scream. There is no one to hear you." Emeline felt a terrible thrust of fear. He was right. "Nod your head, if you promise not to scream, and I shall drop my hand." She nodded vigorously.

Standing before her—as if he had either descended from heaven or sprung from hell—stood a tall figure in a long dark cloak. Emeline did not cry out.

"Are you a Confederate sympathizer?" he asked.

She looked at him, realized that he was a Federal naval officer, and didn't answer. He asked her again more kindly. Now she heard the traces of his Southern accent, and she managed a faint, "Yes, sir."

"You don't know me, ma'am. I have relatives in New Bern, and I came to warn the Confederates. The Union commander plans to burn the Trent River Bridge and attack the town."

Emeline gave a shocked gasp. "When?"

"In twenty-four hours, perhaps less."

"Where, sir?"

He hesitated but only for a moment. "Our forces will go ashore at the mouth of Slocum's Creek." And with that he wheeled and strode off into the darkness. In a few minutes she heard the creak of oarlocks somewhere out on the water.

Suddenly she found herself at the edge of a dim yellow circle of light. As she stumbled and almost fell, her foot encountered something far too yielding to be a log or a piece of driftwood. Sputtering, almost out, a lantern lay overturned on the ground. When she turned up the flame, she was barely able to stifle her scream.

She had stumbled upon a man's body. The eyes were wide open and staring directly up at her. It was a Yankee seaman who was very dead. Had he encountered the officer in the long dark cloak and become suspicious of his presence here? She realized that the Union officer had been searching for someone to take his warning to the Confederates, seen her, and waited until she reached this desolate spot.

Death and intrigue sometimes went hand in hand, she thought. It was a night when a chance encounter was pointing her life toward a great destiny and perhaps great danger. She shuddered.

Then Emeline straightened her shoulders, and it was as if a more determined young woman emerged from within the girlish figure. Now she had a mission. She must reach the Confederates with the Union officer's warning. She would take her father's swiftest horse.

Reaching her home at Calico Creek, she hurried to the stable. "Saddle Duke," she called out to the stable boy and then headed for the house to change into her riding habit. The dark green jacket set off her creamy skin and auburn hair. As she mounted the big roan a voice at her elbow suddenly spoke and someone grasped the reins.

"Where do you think you're going?"

For a moment she was afraid it was her father. But it was only her brother, Levi, whose voice already was taking on a similar deep timbre.

The Spy of Morehead City

"Tell Papa I left to visit Mary Belle at New Bern and will be back in the late afternoon."

"Emeline, where are you *really* going?"

"I'll tell you later. It's an emergency." He squeezed her arm affectionately, "Good luck, Em." She turned the horse toward New Bern.

She had not ridden far when a voice shouted out of the blackness, "Halt!" A rider cantered toward her, and she was terrified that it might be a Yankee. It was only a Confederate picket who let her go. The moon was brighter now, the trail easier to follow.

Her horse whinnied, catching the scent of wood smoke from camp fires borne on the fresh salty wind from the sea, and she asked herself, Our boys or Yankees? She began to keep to the center of the trail so Duke's feet wouldn't snap the twigs of the brush at either side. She prayed he wouldn't whinny again, for though they were safely downwind, if the men who had built the fire didn't hear her, their horses would. Suddenly Duke whinnied and reared up in fear. Emeline began to talk soothingly, reaching down to pat him. As she did her hand touched that of a man.

Terrified, she forced herself to speak boldly.

"Take your hand off my horse's bridle," she said, her voice curt. "You're endangering the lives of our men with the smoke from your fire."

It was another Confederate sentry. "One of our girls are you? Well, you might be right, ma'am, if the Yankees weren't miles away from here."

"Not so far as you might think," replied Emeline less sharply, for now that she could see the face of the soldier,

Outer Banks of North Carolina

her fear subsided. He looked more like a boy with his small pinched features and beardless face. His butternut uniform was shabby, and he wore no overcoat to protect him from the cold. Feeling a sudden wave of sympathy for him, she reached into the saddlebag and gave him her brother's old woolen gloves. He accepted them gratefully.

"How far am I from the commanding officer's headquarters?" she asked, explaining that she had an urgent message to deliver.

"'Bout three miles, ma'am. When you reach the big oak take the fork where the trail bears left."

The clouds thinned, and now she could see the moon—a pale galleon sailing in a wispy trough of clouds. Temporarily the forest trail was drenched by its light. When she reached the fork she was challenged again, this time by an officer who rode out from among a group of Confederates and reined his horse in beside hers. Before he could speak, Emeline demanded to be taken to the commanding officer.

"I'm sorry, but Colonel Taylor doesn't have time to see you. He's much too busy," replied the young captain in a courteous but firm voice.

"If he wishes to avoid another disaster like Roanoke Island, he will find time to see me." The captain gave her a hard stare, and she flushed realizing her words had been impertinent. But she was tired of the obstacles in her path. Observing her determined gaze and her beauty, the officer smiled and motioned for her to follow. He introduced himself, and together they rode through the woods to the commander's tent, receiving permission to enter.

Colonel Taylor listened with interest, and then his

grey eyes bored into hers as if trying to read her true character. "You might be able to help us a great deal. Would you be willing to gather more information for the Confederacy?"

Surprised and tired, she hesitated.

"Think about it," he said. "I'm not asking for an immediate answer."

"The answer is yes. I can tell you that now."

"Before I accept that, young lady, I warn you that if you are caught with any message on your person, you will be executed as a spy."

"The Yankees would shoot me, sir?"

"Hang you or shoot you, one or the other. The fact you're a woman would be no protection."

"Then I must keep from being caught," she said gravely, and he nodded.

"I'm not able to ride this far often without attracting attention. How could we solve that?"

"Let me suggest you relay information to your fellow townsman Captain Josiah Pender, or to whomever he recommends." Emeline nodded, her large black eyes shining with excitement. Before she left the colonel insisted that she have a glass of sherry and a biscuit. He poured the wine himself from a Waterford decanter, and she sat for a few minutes sipping it before the fire while he asked friendly questions about her home and family.

Then his mood changed and he shook his head. "Well, war clouds continue to darken over our coast." He glanced at his pocket watch. "You're tired, young lady. McRae, accompany Miss Emeline back to Morehead City, or as far as you deem wise."

McRae did as he was ordered, charming his attractive

companion on the way. He was a Virginian and knew many important people in Richmond and Washington. Emeline was fascinated by the stories of intrigue. In the capital city top officials in Lincoln's cabinet still socialized with those who secretly sympathized with the Confederacy. She had heard her father and his friends talk of how a woman spy had brought information to General Beauregard of the route the Yankees would take to Manassas and Centreville. Because of her the Confederate victory became a rout, and Beauregard boasted that he had known not only who the commander would be but also how many enemy soldiers there would be, to a man!

Emeline Pigott listened enthralled. Yes! She wanted to be a spy.

Not only intelligent and fearless, she also possessed a sense of destiny. Convinced that the purpose of her meeting that night with the officer beside the marsh had led her to this opportunity to help the Confederacy, she acted without hesitating.

Two days later Emeline waked to the steady roar of heavy cannon fire. It came from the direction of New Bern, and she knew the Federal fleet had gone up the Neuse River to attack just below the town. She remembered Captain McRae. His face had been in her thoughts often. They had discussed how he might come to town dressed as a civilian and serve as a contact himself between her and Colonel Taylor. But in a small village the presence of a stranger was always suspect.

On Friday Emeline spent most of the morning doing needle work, but it was not cross-stitch or embroidery.

The Spy of Morehead City

She was cleverly sewing pockets into one of her petticoats. Noon came and she heard her father's footsteps on the porch. "Our men have retreated across the Trent Bridge, and Burnside has captured New Bern," he announced, his face grave. Emeline paled. The Confederates had not been trapped, but New Bern's loss was a great blow. The entire Beaufort-Morehead area was now sealed off from the outside world.

At their rear the Yankees held New Bern. In front of them the Federal blockade was on the sound side and at sea. Emeline knew everyone would be closely watched, and that included her.

The Union forces would undoubtedly attack Fort Macon next—but when? It was important to find out. The Pigott home soon became a popular place for social gatherings overflowing with Union general Burnside's men. Emeline drifted from one group of officers to another, chatting animatedly. Major John Allen from Rhode Island grew quite infatuated with her. He found her knowledgeable about politics, a lively conversationalist, and a good listener. She was always surrounded by admirers, and the major sometimes became impatient to be with her alone.

On the night of April 18 an especially merry evening was in progress at the Pigott house, and Emeline was forced to conceal her worry over the greatly increased Union activity she had noticed. Major Allen made an effort to separate her from the young men in the parlor and take her out on the front porch. This once she permitted him to do so.

Tonight his jealousy served her purpose well. He

guarded his tongue less carefully than usual, and when she asked if he would like to join a group for a picnic, his reply intrigued her.

"I will be delighted if I may be your escort." He paused, abruptly, adding, "That is, if it is not between the twenty-third and twenty-fifth."

Hoping he would interpret the sudden sparkle he may have seen in her eyes as pleasure at his invitation she replied, "I shall be honored."

He had inadvertently supplied her with the probable date that the attack on Fort Macon would be launched. She knew it was not far off from the supplies the Federal commissaries were laying in, from merchant friends who were Union sympathizers, and from a wily peddler who traded with the enemy. Best of all, a venturesome farm lad had told her brother Levi where all the Federal batteries and rifle pits were, and from this information, she and Levi sketched the location of each installation.

The next morning, dressing her hair with great care, Emeline took a piece of thin paper upon which she had recorded the information, folded it into a small square of dark silk, and concealed it beneath a chignon of her gleaming auburn locks. She was acquainted with a boy named Robert Stanton who was on duty at Fort Macon. Robert was her contact with the peddler, and she had sent word through him to the peddler that she had "something important for him."

As she strolled along Evans Street, she nodded good-morning to Cornelius Hill, an influential and affluent merchant well known for his friendliness with the enemy. Her courier, a quiet lad of fourteen with dark curly hair, was to meet her at some point on the street. He had

The Spy of Morehead City

proven reliable, and she had even sent Captain McRae several messages through him. As she passed the youth, she was to drop one of the books she carried. She would quickly slip him the note as he returned the book to her.

Emeline touched her hair with a deft feminine gesture, as if to practice how she would remove the message. She was always poised, so that even a close friend would not have detected that she was more nervous and apprehensive than usual.

She saw the boy approaching at a maddeningly slow pace. Was something wrong? He was walking more purposefully now. They were about to pass when one of the books slipped from beneath her arm to the ground. She gave her hair a pat in a quick movement of vexation, then with a smile reached for the book the boy had picked up and said a pleasant "Thank you." For the briefest instant her hand touched his. Another message damaging to the Yankees was on its way.

There were many other occasions like this—moments fraught with danger, but destiny and good luck seemed to go hand in hand for Emeline. Just as exciting were the nights Captain McRae, in one disguise or another, appeared at the door of the house on Calico Creek. Emeline began to realize that it was more than messages that excited her during these visits. When they became engaged in the spring of 1863 she felt that once more destiny was at work in her life. Her encounter with the Union officer beside the marsh had led to the opportunity to help the Confederacy; then came the meeting with Captain Stokes McRae. Sometimes in moments of reflection she was able to see a pattern in everything that happened to her.

Outer Banks of North Carolina

As the war continued she was a combination of spy and angel of mercy, repeatedly smuggling mail or food or warm clothing through the enemy lines during New Bern's occupation by Federal troops. Her activities took her not only as far away as Kinston but half-way across the state.

One day in mid-February, 1865, while Union vessels were bombarding Fort Anderson to the South near Wilmington, Emeline had an important message to send and supplies to be smuggled to Confederate soldiers. Before she left her home she filled the secret pockets sewn into the petticoat beneath her voluminous skirt, placing in them toothbrushes, two pocket knives, a shirt, two pairs of pants, gloves, and candy. To her joy she had also managed to find room for a pair of sturdy boots.

As she strolled along Evans Street, no one could have imagined that this lovely woman was a walking supply depot. But of a much more serious nature was the copy of a Union order she had concealed among the shining auburn coils of her hair. Once again she was expecting her courier to appear at any moment. She caught a glimpse of the peddler who often supplied her with news of Union plans.

He was watching her, and with a sense of foreboding she averted her eyes. Then, still feeling his gaze upon her back, she turned, and he looked quickly away. She usually did not experience such gloomy premonitions. Pausing to stare in the window of a millinery shop, she wondered about the peddler's trustworthiness for the first time. When money changes hands, loyalties sometimes change, too, she thought.

At that moment, two Union soldiers who had been

looking into a store window near her abruptly turned to face her.

"Miss Emeline, I believe," said one of them. They flanked her on either side.

"How do you know my name?"

"Everyone knows you around here, Miss Emeline," jeered one of the men, taking her arm in a gesture that was much too familiar. He was a heavy-set sergeant with straw-colored hair and bold eyes. "You know a good many of our officers, don't you?"

She shook his hand off her arm angrily and did not reply.

"Now, ma'am, don't act that a'way. We'll all become good friends where you're going."

"I doubt that! What are you talking about?"

"You're goin' to pay a visit to the Federal prison at New Bern," he said, sneering at her. "Now, ain't it a shame for a pretty lady like you to be tryin' to help the Rebs and gettin' in such bad trouble?"

She suddenly recalled the colonel's warning not to carry written information on her person. "You risk being hanged or shot as a spy," he had said. Fear, sharp as a knife, pierced her as she remembered the folded square of paper in her hair. But her gaze remained steady.

"I'll have to go home and get my clothing first."

"Sorry, ma'am," said the pleasant-faced young corporal, speaking up for the first time. "We will send someone to tell your family, ma'am, so's they can bring your things." Emeline could imagine her parents' anger and shock. As for Levi—she only hoped he was not at home when the soldier arrived. He might be furious enough to kill him!

The sergeant was angry. "'Sorry, ma'am. Yes, ma'am. No, ma'am.' Do you have to talk to her so damn polite, corporal?" he barked. "You sound like one of the Rebs yourself."

"Sorry, sir," replied the corporal.

"Just remember this girl's been tryin' to get our men killed!"

The lieutenant and the sergeant were helping Emeline into an army supply wagon when Cornelius Hill came out of the barber shop. Seeing them, his pale blue eyes registered shock, and he pressed his lips tightly together.

"What's going on?" he asked the soldiers.

"It's off to the Federal prison at New Bern for her, sir," said the sergeant. Hill looked at Emeline in surprise, seemed ready to ask a question but thought better of it. Instead, he offered—"for the lady's comfort"—the loan of his carriage and coachman.

"You're Colonel Rodman's friend, aren't you, sir?" the sergeant asked. Rodman was an influential Union officer. "I guess it's all right then." Hill's face reddened under Emeline's gaze. He turned and gave some instructions to his coachman but did not accompany Emeline. When Hill's shiny yellow carriage with its two sleek black horses drew up before the prison, Emeline stared at the sergeant haughtily.

"I refuse to leave this carriage until the commander comes out and tells me why I have been brought here!"

Even the doughty sergeant was reluctant to drag her forcibly from the coach. He and the corporal walked a few paces from the carriage to decide what to do. Emeline

The Spy of Morehead City

played for time. She swiftly withdrew the message from her hair, thrust it into her mouth, and swallowed it. When the men returned she pretended to have changed her mind and obediently accompanied her captors. But the commander soon found nothing could be learned from questioning her.

Despite her protests he called in a local woman to search her person. The result was the amazing collection of items from the pockets of her petticoat but nothing that constituted a hanging offense. Her questioners found no evidence at all to execute Emeline, but the commander knew she was guilty. He also knew more subtle ways of getting rid of a spy.

The days of Emeline's imprisonment dragged slowly by. There seemed no hope that she would be freed. One night she wakened to find the room suffused with a heavy, sweet odor. She had nursed too many sick soldiers not to recognize chloroform. Seized by panic, she knew her captors were trying to send her into that deeper sleep from which there is no return.

Her fingers searched the molding around the window. Finding a crack with a rag protruding from it, she soon discovered a bottle of chloroform sitting on the window ledge. She managed to nudge it off into the bushes below, and pressing her face against the crack, Emeline sat breathing the lifegiving fresh air for the rest of the night.

Dawn arrived, and she heard footsteps in the hall. It was the hostile sergeant. He called her name, but she chose not to reply. "I hope the poor girl's all right," he said to a guard with feigned concern. The key rattled in the door. When he entered the room and saw she was fine, the mixture of surprise and disappointment on his face was unmistakable.

"You really are vermin. Get out!" Emeline said furiously. He left, but she knew this would not be the last attempt on her life. Tears began to stream down her cheeks for the first time since she had been in prison, and she lay on the cot sobbing. Her friends had tried to help free her but with no success. She might die in this place and never see her sweetheart again. Then a plan came to her and she began to think very calmly. Could she bribe one of the guards to deliver a message to Cornelius Hill?

Emeline was fortunate that the young soldier who had been so polite to her at her arrest stopped at her cell. She asked him if he would carry the message, and he nodded in a kind fashion. Nor would he take any money for delivering the note. "No trouble, ma'am." He would find an opportunity to give it to Cornelius Hill.

At noon there was a knock on her door. It was only the guard with her lunch. Was the food safe to eat? She didn't know and was afraid to touch it. Two o'clock, two-thirty, three o'clock passed, but no one came. Her anxiety increased. Would the note reach Mr. Hill in time? She had no idea when the next attempt on her life would occur—perhaps tonight.

At a quarter to four there was a sharp rap on the door, and there stood the sergeant.

"Someone to see you."

"Who?"

"You'll learn soon enough" was his gruff reply.

She heard footsteps and saw the portly form of Cornelius Hill standing behind the soldier in the corridor. The sergeant lingered to overhear the conversation, but Hill glowered at him and off he sauntered. Emeline wasted no time on pleasantries.

"Mr. Hill," she said in low tones, "what I say may not be good to hear, but I think it will be for your benefit and that of the others." He interrupted, "The others?" His voice was apprehensive.

"Yes. I know of traitorous acts committed by some of the most prominent men in our area, and I must warn you that if I am not released by nightfall, someone outside the prison is ready to name names."

Hill spluttered. "What do you mean? I haven't done anything!"

"What about paying fishermen to take supplies to Union blockade runners?"

"Ridiculous!"

"And then there was the written message on Confederate troop movements sent by you through . . ."

Now Hill's eyes showed fear. "All right! What do you want in return for not divulging any of this? Lies, of course."

"I must be taken out of this prison and returned home before another night passes." His face showed doubt. "Shall I give you more?" she asked.

He paled. "My God, no! I must go now."

Emeline sat down to do her needlework and read the Bible. Her supper tray went untouched. Would her scheme work? She did have the information, but she had no one who knew of these things outside the prison. Even if she did, how could she get in touch with that person? The only advantage she possessed was that since she had been able to get a message to him, Hill probably thought that she could easily contact someone else.

She wondered what her fate would be if she was not released. She could think of other means that could be used to kill her—means that could make her death appear accidental—and she dreaded the approach of darkness.

Losing hope of Hill's effecting her release that day, as the late afternoon light faded she sat down in the single chair in her cell. Her shoulders drooped with despair.

"Miss Emeline! Miss Emeline!" A voice shouted to her through the cell door. "Get ready!"

"Get ready?"

"Yes. You're going home."

Her ruse had worked! A half hour later Emeline walked out through the big doors at the prison entrance into her father's arms. He had tears in his eyes, but Levi had a mile-wide grin and gave her a bear hug. She was on her way back to Calico Creek.

At a place called Appomattox, Virginia, peace arrived with the tender green leaves of spring. Across the beautiful rolling countryside stretched lines of rag-clad Confederates, "so weak that we could hardly stand," said one of them later. Before them were rows of well-fed, well-clad Federal troops.

Lee and Grant discussed the terms of the surrender in a home near the courthouse. As Union officers stood and watched, General Lee wrote out the formal surrender agreement. Before the two generals parted, Grant acceded to Lee's request that the Confederates be permitted to take their mounts with them since the individual soldiers, rather than the army, owned them. When they reached home many would need the horses who had served them so faithfully in battle to help plow the ground and plant spring crops. Grant also ordered the Union quartermaster to feed the hungry Confederates, whose half-starved condition shocked the Union troops.

Emeline waited expectantly, but Captain McRae did not return. Then a ragged Confederate soldier, a young lieutenant, drove up one evening in a wagon. He had served under the captain. "Bravest officer I ever knew. I worshiped that man," he exclaimed.

"Was he sent to a Northern prison?" Emeline questioned, her face lighting up with hope.

"Ma'am, I'm sorry." The former soldier could not look at her and his voice broke. "He died at Gettysburg. I was with him. After the surrender I went back for him. His skeleton was still right where he fell."

In the wagon was a pine box, and despite her reluctance to do so, Emeline examined the remains. Tears streamed down her face. A bullet had once grazed Stokes McRae's left wrist, shearing off a small bit of bone. She wasn't sure she noticed evidence of that wound, and despite the North Carolina buttons on his uniform, she thought the dead man could be someone else. But she made sure that he received proper burial. His resting place was her family cemetery, and on the marker "The Unknown Soldier" was engraved.

Now the hopeful spirit that had sustained her through the ordeal of her imprisonment was gone. Sometimes in later years she would walk down to the family cemetery at dusk—a small, straight-backed figure striding purposefully along—and leave a rose on the grave.

In the will read after her death she requested that she

be buried "beside the unknown soldier." She may have had second thoughts: perhaps the grave really did belong to Stokes McRae.

Down through the years, when the mist rises and swirls at night, the figures of a Confederate soldier and a young woman in Civil War–era dress are sometimes seen in the springtime strolling along the road near the point. Romantics believe they are the apparitions of Stokes McRae and Emeline—their destiny to be together fulfilled at last in death.

ooo

Some sources place Stokes McRae's death as occurring in Gettysburg; others believe it was during the final campaign in the Shenandoah Valley.

Petersburg—
From mid-June, 1864, through March, 1865, a number of engagements were fought south and west of Petersburg, Virginia. In March, 1865, General Robert E. Lee's attack on Fort Stedman failed to force General Ulysses S. Grant back. His last supply line cut, Lee was forced to evacuate Petersburg on April 2, 1865.
Petersburg National Battlefield is at Petersburg,
Virginia, twenty-six miles south of Richmond on
Interstate 85.

○○○

THE TIMELY APPARITIONS

Petersburg, Virginia

It had been a disastrous day for the Confederacy. One tragic blow after another had fallen. Lieutenant General A. P. Hill had been killed trying to close a breach in the Confederate line near Hatcher's Run, west of the city of Petersburg; Fort Gregg had been overwhelmed; and in the final battle of the day, Federal forces had cut the tracks of the South Side Railroad.

That night in the darkness, regiment after regiment of ragged, worn Confederates began marching out of Petersburg. Their orders from General Lee were to evacuate the city, cross to the north side of the Appomattox River, and begin the trek westward. The men were tired and dispirited from the day's fighting. Some would probably have deserted when the orders to march came had it not been for their love of Lee. The evacuation meant the end for the city of Petersburg.

Arriving Union officers headquartered in Centre Hill,

Petersburg, Virginia

one of the city's most beautiful homes, built by Robert Bolling in 1823. Four days after the officers entered Petersburg, Lincoln visited General George L. Hartsuff at Centre Hill to tour the city that had been the Union's long sought objective.

An officer belonging to Hartsuff's staff, not feeling well, had decided to spend the evening in his room. He was alone on the second floor—Hartsuff and the other Federal officers having left to attend a dinner party more than an hour before—when he heard the door to the office beneath him opening. He started to rise and investigate. Then it occurred to him that one of the men had probably come back to get something that had been forgotten or even to fetch something for the general. Again he settled himself in his bed and looked at his watch. Since it was 7:30 P.M. on the 24th of January, it had been dark for more than an hour. Although he had convinced himself that one of the officers had returned for something, he heard hinges creak loudly and the sound of a door thrust open with such force that it struck the wall. This noise was followed by the sound of marching footsteps and the clank of weapons.

The Union officer seized his revolver and rushed out into the hall, gazing agitatedly in both directions. The hall was empty, but in regular rhythm, throughout the entire house, he heard the distinct tread of marching feet. Beads of perspiration began to form on his forehead. He resisted the impulse to dash back into his room, slam the door, and bolt the lock. The footsteps in the hall were loudest right beside him. He stood there trembling.

He heard the marchers' heavy *tramp–tramp–tramp* going down the stairs, boots scraping each tread as they

The Timely Apparitions

went striding across the floor of the entrance hall. Finally the front door slammed. By now the men must be out of the house and in the street below. Rushing over to the windows of his room he threw open the velvet drapes and stared out. The yellow glare of the gas street lamps illuminated an empty street.

According to author L. B. Taylor, Jr., who wrote *The Ghosts of Richmond . . . And Nearby Environs,* so regular was the procession that owners of Centre Hill invited friends and neighbors in to experience the event. The phenomena of the Ghost Brigade was an annual occurrence each January 24th at 7:30 P.M., and the sound of it could be heard throughout the Hill. In her book Marguerite DuPont Lee describes the sequence of events as they occurred: "On that day of the year, the clock pointing to the half hour, the door leading into the office was heard to open. Then came a noise such as of a regiment of soldiers marching! The clank of sabers suggested the occupation of those tramping along the passage; up the stairs and into a room over the office the footsteps came. After about twenty minutes the sound was again heard descending the steps, crossing the hall, then the slamming of a door and all was quiet."

People in the neighborhood associate Centre Hill with yet another eerie tale—the specter of a woman who appears in the upstairs window just above the front door. She was first seen in the late 1800s, when the mansion was a private home.

One day a small boy who lived there said, "Mother, who is the pretty lady who holds my hand and talks to me sometimes when I'm in bed at night?"

Petersburg, Virginia

"Are you sure you aren't imagining her, my dear?
What does she look like?"

"I'm not sure but I think she's pretty, and, mother, I
can see right through her!"

His mother was, of course, amazed, and when the child
told her that "the lady plays beautiful music," the mother
recalled that sometimes she thought she heard the melo-
deon strike up some familiar air. When she looked in the
room seconds later, no one was there, and she hesitated
to speak of these experiences to other members of the
family.

A former resident of the house insists that the lady
has her own bedroom, and angrily jerks the covers off
her bed if anyone sleeps in it. But most often she is seen
at dusk. Some passers-by automatically glance up when
they come near Centre Hill, for they say that the lady
always gazes out of the same upstairs window.

ooo

Centre Hill is now owned by the City of Petersburg
and is open to the public.

According to the Albany *Evening Times,* when the last of April comes, railroad men on the right-of-way of the New York Central claim they see a phantom train with flags and long black streamers traveling slowly through the night. Its brass fittings gleam with a strange phosphorescence in the moonlight, and the shades are drawn. It is the annual reappearance of Lincoln's funeral train. The route of the impressive, bedraped train covered seventeen hundred miles from Washington, D.C., north and then across the plains to Springfield, Illinois. Three hundred mourners rode in the Pullman cars, and at every stop crowds of grieving Americans thronged the train.

ooo

THE NIGHT TRAIN PASSES

Near Albany, New York

Normally he would have been with his wife on their wedding anniversary. Tonight was different.

When Carter Strothers saw the blonde-haired little girl, her flushed face lying against the pillow, he knew immediately that he had been wise to make a house call. Under most circumstances he would have advised her mother to bring her to his office in the morning. The girl's home was a thirty-minute drive for the doctor, but something the mother said—he wasn't even sure exactly what—touched off a warning in his brain: danger.

Lisa's face and body were feverish, and the thermometer he had pulled from his worn black bag, then shaken down energetically before placing it under her tongue, registered 105 degrees. He remembered his first years of practice realizing that she might have died then but not

Near Albany, New York

voicing such thoughts. She had a full-blown case of pneumonia, and he felt for his hypodermic and penicillin. He had been the first of the doctors in his small town near Albany, New York, to begin using it.

A short time later he was backing his pale blue Buick out of the drive and was on his way home. It was the last week of April, 1965. Tonight he and Anne, whom he had met just after she had graduated from New York University, would be married three decades—exceptionally happy years. Some of his friends' wives had pushed their husbands to leave these little towns between New York and Albany and develop practices in New York City. He would have hated that sort of impersonality and pressure.

His son went to West Point, and they saw him often. A daughter followed in her mother's footsteps and attended NYU. Even when she was a senior her father worried about her living in the city.

He saw the lights of East Albany in the distance, checked his watch, and wondered if Anne had fallen asleep waiting for him. It was about 10:30. He heard the sound of a train not far away and was surprised to see how slowly it was going. It couldn't be traveling over twenty miles an hour. There was the toll of a bell. He didn't believe he had heard a train bell in years! He pulled up close to the tracks to see it, and he lowered the window. Overhead stars were visible.

The train was only seconds away now, and he noticed two railroad men who stood a few feet away watching.

"Look at the engine. Doesn't that look like the old *Union?*"

"You've got to be crazy!"

The Night Train Passes

"Take a gander at the train and the cars behind it. Ever see anything going so slow?"

Narrowing his eyes, the younger man shook his head. "No. Looks like something out of an old picture in a railroad station—or maybe a book."

In the car, Doc Strothers turned his head. The moon was out now, and he could see the train approaching on an open stretch of track. The engine was heavily draped in black with a cowcatcher jutting out in front of it. The stack blew silvery smoke puffs up into the air from its wide mouth. He couldn't see the engineer, but behind the cab he caught a glimpse of logs for refueling. He stared at the wheels which had an almost hypnotic effect upon him as the train crept toward him, its speed not exceeding twenty miles an hour.

The engine was pulling only nine cars. The fittings of the coaches were polished until what must have been brass gleamed like bright silver in the moonlight. Here and there were small flags. Each coach was draped with black and had black streamers, and as the second car from the last passed, the doctor saw the most amazing sight of all. Through the train window he stared in at a group of blue-coated men. They were gathered around something. He leaned forward straining to see until in the midst of them he was able to see clearly the object which held their attention. It was a casket! He felt perspiration break out on his forehead.

Suddenly he realized how hushed and still everything was—not a sound, almost as if the train were rolling over a soft carpet. He looked in his rearview mirror to see if he saw an automobile. No. The two men stood near the track watching, not moving. It was impossible to believe

Near Albany, New York

that a train could make no noise whatsoever. But that was the way it was. The night was as quiet as the grave. With an almost electric shock it came to him that this was a funeral train. The incredibly slow speed, the black decor, the military men—everything was in honor of a very important person, someone as important as a president of the United States.

He rested his elbow on the window sill, and his fingers touched the chrome edge of the small pane that opened outward. In an effort to view the train better he leaned his head out a little. It was then that he felt a stream of air blow past his face and hand. He saw the two railroad men step back startled, their faces white in the moonlight.

Finally the last car moved along the track before him. During all the time that the train had been passing, there had not been a sound. Dr. Carter Strothers looked

The train made no noise whatsoever.

The Night Train Passes

at his watch and was surprised to see that for the first time during the six months he had owned it, the watch had stopped.

It was not until he had picked up the Albany *Evening Times* one evening several years later that he read this story:

> On the right-of-way of the New York Central, sandhouse men, section hands, and track-walkers tell the ghost story of the phantom train. They say it is Lincoln's funeral train. The train is pulled by a brand new engine. Put on at New York, *The Union* pulled the cars across New York state and on to Springfield, Illinois. Railroad men who have seen the train say:
>
> "Late at night, in the last week of the month of April, the air along the track becomes keen—chill. But on either side it is warm and still. *The Union* and the eight cars travel noiselessly past. If a real train should go by at the same time, the noise of the real train hushes as if the phantom train is rolling over it or replacing it in time and space. As the phantom train passes clocks and watches stop.

Now Carter Strothers understood his experience that night beside the track of the New York Central.

Whether the event that happened in May, 1863, at Bat-chelder's Creek, near Kinston, was a natural phenomenon or fell in the realm of the supernatural did not matter. The Union soldiers would never forget it.

"GHOST" FRIGHTENS NEW ENGLANDERS

Near Kinston, North Carolina

"It is not to be supposed that the men forming the 25th Massachusetts Regiment, educated as they were in the schools of New England, and possessing all the general intelligence marking the New England character," modestly writes Captain J. W. Denny, in *American Civil War Battlefield Sketches: Battlefield Echoes*, "had gone down to North Carolina to be frightened by ghosts, owls or live rebels, or that they would be inclined to believe in stories about ghosts, fairies, witches and apparitions."

To continue from the Federal records, "It was the latter part of May 1863 when General J. G. Foster at New Bern received information that Lee was preparing for an offensive across the Potomac and had urgent need for reinforcements from General D. H. Hill's command in North Carolina. This put Hill on the defensive and gave us another chance at the Confederates. Our efforts to whip them at Gum Swamp the month before had failed."

Foster was eager to move inland and reach the Atlantic and North Carolina Railroad, and his first move was to order Colonel Richter Jones to head for Gum Swamp

"Ghost" Frightens New Englanders

and try to surround the enemy. Gum Swamp was a Confederate outpost about eight miles below Kinston, which was the objective. Two of the regiments that reinforced Colonel Jones were the Massachusetts 46th and the 25th. The plan was for five regiments to converge upon the Confederate outpost at daybreak and make a joint attack from the front and the rear.

The 25th Massachusetts had marched all day and into the night and had halted for a rest. It was an exceptionally dark, moonless night, and they were making their way through pine woods to Batchelder's Creek. The column's aim was to go through the woods as quietly as possible in order not to attract the attention of enemy pickets.

While the battalion stood halted in the road, something struck the flank of Company K which had the advance. It came like the rushing of a mighty wind, and suddenly the company opened to the right and left, and just as suddenly the men were in heaps in the ditches on either side of the road. There was no order or regard for rank. Captains and lieutenants, sergeants and corporals, men from the front ranks and men from the rear were all indiscriminately heaped together like piles of jack straws.

As Captain Denny described it, "Each man's hair stood erect upon his head like quills from a fretted porcupine. The men scrambled up out of the ditch and regrouped. They hurried, for the men of the 46th Massachusetts regiment were now coming up close upon their rear. No sooner had they gotten themselves into some semblance of order when, to their astonishment, there was the same strange rushing sound, and the men of the

Near Kinston, North Carolina

46th Massachusetts Regiment dove for the ditches in as complete and chaotic disorder as they had done."

Neither the sound nor the startled fright of these two regiments has ever been explained. There could have been no more precipitate flight had Colonel Mosby and his men suddenly appeared on one of their well known ambuscades, firing their revolvers at close range into the midst of them.

The sudden rising of a wind and its quick cessation can be awesome and has sometimes been associated with spirits. Occurring twice in rapid succession in the same place and felt by two separate regiments of men seems to be unheard of. Ghost or not, it was an unforgettable experience for the New England regiments.

When Gilbert Bates arrived in the U.S. capital, the Washington monument was just being built. It was only a pile of stones with little indication of its grandeur to come. But George Washington would certainly have understood this former Union soldier who may have saved a president from being impeached.

OOO

THE VICTOR'S WALK

Edgerton, Wisconsin

His breath rose in the cold air as he broke the ice on the water troughs and fed the animals. There was not much else for Gilbert Bates to do on the farm this morning. The spacious family farmhouse here at Albion, Wisconsin, where he had grown up was not far from Edgerton. Snow had fallen during the night, followed by a light rain, and his wagon wheels crunched noisily along through a sparkling crust of ice that November morning of 1867.

He enjoyed driving into town for supplies and the sociability the excursion provided. At the general store he would always find several friends exchanging stories as they sat warming themselves on cold mornings around the black potbellied stove. The war was still the topic of much conversation, and like most of the other men Bates had served in the Union Army. He had been a sergeant.

Bates, a Democrat, had just settled himself to toast his feet when in came a Radical Republican friend of his and sat down near him. As the sergeant expected, his friend began his usual tirade about what traitors to the country Southerners were, and that they should be punished. Fur began to fly. As the argument became heated, others pitched in.

"Gilbert, those Southerners are still rebels. They're worse now than during the war, and they hate the Union flag."

"That's ridiculous," said Bates.

"Oh it is, ay. Why, no man dares to show the flag anywhere in the South, unless in the presence of our occupying soldiers."

Bates's face flushed with irritation. "You're all wrong," he said. "I could carry the flag myself from the Mississippi all over the rebel states—alone and un-armed."

"You'd be lucky to get back alive. I say traitors don't change."

"They're Americans just like us," said Bates, who had been with the First Wisconsin Heavy Artillery. "I'll bet I could walk right along the route Sherman marched to the sea, and nobody would touch me."

There was much exclaiming and headshaking over that statement, and the entire group decided to take him up on the bet.

"I just want to see you walk from Vicksburg, Missis-sippi, to Washington, D.C." said the Radical Republican.

"You've got to go unarmed," said another; "that's a condition."

"And alone!" interposed a third. "No bodyguard."

"He'll never get back!" said the shopkeeper.

Someone asked Bates if he planned to carry a large sum of money.

"I'm not going to carry *any* money or accept any along

The Victor's Walk

the way. I plan to live on Southern hospitality," replied Bates.

"Why they'll put out a banquet spread for you," somebody jeered. At this the men haw-hawed. Everyone knew much of the land had been devastated and parts of the South were close to famine.

"That'll be suicide. I'll bet you never get back," said the Republican. That snowy morning Gilbert Bates and his friends sat around the stove and decided all the terms of the bet. Bates was to begin his walk at Vicksburg, Mississippi, and arrive in Washington, D.C., on or before the Fourth of July, 1868. If he arrived in the capital, unharmed and with his flag intact, his Radical Republican friend was to give Bates's family one dollar for each day of his trip. The wager became the talk of the state, and before Bates could leave, several cities had offered him a flag to carry.

"I won't need it," Bates told them confidently. "Vicksburg will provide me with a flag."

Since it was winter he dressed in warm clothes and wore heavy walking boots. On the train to Vicksburg he met a salesman from Kentucky, and in the course of the conversation he told him about his mission to prove the brotherhood of men both North and South. Bates was thirty, with square shoulders, deep-set blue-gray eyes, and a courteous manner. The salesman was so impressed that when the train reached Vicksburg he insisted on putting his friend up at the Prentiss House.

Next morning Gilbert Bates heard the sound of voices outside and couldn't imagine what was happening. Staring out the window he saw a crowd of people gathered in front of the house. He bathed and dressed immediately and went out on the porch, where, to his relief and surprise, he found the mayor along with a committee of prominent citizens come to welcome him. After getting him settled in the hotel, his friend had visited the mayor and told him about Bates's arrival.

Among the crowd was a lady representing a women's organization. Coming forward, she extended her hand to welcome the visitor, announcing that a flag was being made for him to carry.

"It will be ready in three more days, and then we shall have a presentation ceremony before you leave Vicksburg."

The former sergeant could not appear on the streets of Vicksburg without having ordinary citizens and fellow veterans of the war come up to shake his hand. Three days after Bates's meeting with the mayor, a band arrived at the Prentiss House, bearing ahead of them the Stars and Stripes. Five feet long and three feet wide, it waved in the breeze. Tears filled the sergeant's eyes, for he knew that the women who had made this flag had only a few years before put their hearts into sewing the Stars and Bars.

"And we have something else for you," said the mayor, presenting Sergeant Bates with a beautiful velvet uniform. It bore his regimental insignia! The clothes in which he had traveled were packed up and sent to Illinois. The young blond flag-bearer was an impressive figure in his fine uniform. As he headed out of Vicksburg in the direction of Jackson, he was followed by a band playing "Tramp, tramp, tramp, the boys are marching." And a triumphal procession of city fathers on horseback

The Victor's Walk

preceded thousands of townspeople who traveled both in carriages and on foot toward the monument to Generals Pemberton (C.S.A.) and Grant (U.S.A.).

When Bates reached the summit of a little hill, he turned to wave his banner, and as he did the crowd gave one round of cheers after another, until, Bates wrote in his diary, the noise "almost awakened the dead echoes of the cannon that had roared about this spot in 1863." Hearing the sound of the band fading as his companions turned back toward town, he pursued his way alone with a sense of sadness at leaving.

On his way to the village of Bovina the sky began to darken and snow started to fall. By three o'clock when he entered the town, he was chilled to the bone, for the air was raw and cold and it was still snowing. The street was deserted. Houses appeared dark and hostile, and the only person in sight was an old gentleman who approached him and asked, "What are you doing carrying the Union flag around?"

Bates explained and the old gentleman took off his own overcoat and put it around the sergeant's shoulders. Then he stepped back, saluted, and disappeared. The sergeant walked on and by late afternoon he saw a ruined plantation house. He knocked and when the owner came to the door he took Bates's arm and drew him inside, insisting that he sit down before the blazing fire to tell his story over a glass of brandy.

"I have to apologize for the barrenness of my hospitality, sir," said his host, Mr. Cordevant of Kidd's Plantation. "The broken windows and wrecked furniture are Northern improvements." Lifting his hand he said, "No offense meant. We probably would have done the same

At Vicksburg a parade honoring Gilbert Bates
began at the courthouse.

The Victor's Walk

thing, if we'd had the opportunity." Cordevant insisted on giving him a warm supper and a bed for the night.

Next morning he was walking along on his way to Smith Station, and a few miles before he reached his destination, a train stopped beside him. Those aboard had already heard the news—the story of the Yank who was walking from Vicksburg with the Stars and Stripes. Many of the passengers wanted to give him money, which Bates refused, but the conductor pushed some bills into his pocket.

"They're for postage stamps for letters home. You write and tell the North that Southerners are all-fired Americans!"

At Smith Station he found a cheering crowd awaiting him, and he suddenly began laughing. When he was able to stop, he told them how pessimistic friends in Wisconsin had feared he would never return alive—that the Southerners would cut out his heart and trample it on the flag. The crowd roared with laughter.

But the trip was not easy. It was a harsh winter that year in northern Mississippi, and snowfall and rain seemed to accompany the sergeant. The wagon roads were so muddy that he finally began to walk beside the railroad tracks. At every town and whistle-stop crowds assembled to greet him. Once a train stopped and its passengers thronged about him cheering and talking. He walked across swamplands, through pine forests, and over red clay hills. In every town accommodations were provided by local people. Some nights he spent at fine plantations, others in backcountry shacks. He later recalled an Irish farm couple who were especially cordial,

Edgerton, Wisconsin

greeting him as "the bowld boy" and insisting he spend the night in their warm shanty.

In Jackson, the Mississippi capital, Sergeant Bates was the city's honored guest and forced to make a speech about American brotherhood from the balcony of the capitol building.

At a lonely place called Hickory, where Andrew Jackson had once camped, Sergeant Bates stopped for the night at the home of a family named Gray. His arm and shoulder were beginning to give him pain. His feet were sore and his flag was wet. In the middle of the night he waked to the sound of loud masculine voices, and looking out the window of his bedroom, he saw some fifty men milling about in the yard. When they spotted him at the window they began to shout. His heart gave a thud. Was it a lynch mob?

Then he distinguished the sound of fiddles striking up the gay lilting notes of "Arkansas Traveler." Immediately he joined them, and when he appeared one of the men shouted, "Some of us has come forty miles to see you, Sarge!" From a keg, the man dipped a cup of whiskey full to the brim and handed it to Bates, calling out above the hullabaloo of voices, "Here's to the flag!" The sergeant sang and jigged and joked with them, and so it went— this journey of a soldier who loved his flag as a symbol of unity and peace.

At Meridian he was drawn through the streets in an open carriage, flag unfurled, while Southern belles waved their handkerchiefs. *The New York Times* wrote "Joyful multitudes everywhere hail his advance as though it were the advance of an emperor."

One morning, walking along a lonely forest road in

The Victor's Walk

Georgia, he rounded a curve to see a young farmer chopping wood. The farmer had been waiting for him. He told Bates he wanted to extend the hospitality of his home, and the sergeant followed. On their way the farmer stopped at a roadside mount marked with a plain wooden board. Bates wrote in his diary about the encounter and recorded what the farmer said: "'We buried my brother here. He was killed fighting for the Confederacy.' I stood on one side of the grave and he on the other, and we bared our heads. He reached his hand to me across the grave, and I clasped it with deepest emotion while we prayed together."

Bates encountered only one hostile Southern publication, a vitriolic periodical which ran for only two years. Called *The Southern Opinion* and published by H. Rives Pollard in Richmond, Virginia, in one article addressed to Bates the writer declared that South Carolinians should "meet you at the border, welcome your insolent approach and seat you on some tall solitary chimney left by Sherman as a bleak monument of his vandal raid, and then let you wave your rag of oppression." Instead twenty-five Confederate veterans waited at the South Carolina border to escort Sergeant Bates with honor into the state. Bates's arrival coincided with the day that the United States Senate began hearings on whether to impeach President Andrew Johnson for being "too appeasing to the South."

In Columbia, South Carolina, Bates noted in his diary, "Shook hands with every man in Columbia today, I think, and with several more than once!"

A touching incident occurred when he reached Charlotte, North Carolina, and a former Confederate soldier

Edgerton, Wisconsin

greeted him bearing a Union regiment flag. "Sir, I was a soldier under Lee," said young James Orr. "Here is a flag of yours we took after hard fighting and many killed. You have recaptured it, sergeant, without firing a shot. Take it."

In the late afternoon of April 8, 1868, Bates crossed the Richmond and Danville Railroad bridge into the city that had been the capital of the Confederacy. Soon he was making his way with difficulty through a throng of well-wishers who had gathered in front of the Exchange Hotel. That night he waved his flag from the top of the capitol building. It was a peak moment of the march—thousands cheered, church bells pealed.

On April 11 Sergeant Bates entered Washington, and despite the rain there were many onlookers as he marched onto Pennsylvania Avenue at Fourteenth, followed by numerous citizens and a brass band.

The procession walked to the north portico of the White House where President Johnson took his hand and welcomed him with a magnificent banquet in his honor. At the conclusion of the banquet and speech-making, Sergeant Bates met his first significant rebuff—not in the South but in the capital city. Radical Republicans, determined to prevent even a symbol of reconciliation with the South, threw up a succession of obstacles to keep Bates from planting his flag on the dome of the Capitol.

Bates and the procession that followed him finally were forced to hold a ceremony before the pile of stones that was the unfinished Washington Monument. The speaker was the Honorable E. O. Perrin of New York, recently named chief justice of the Supreme Court of Utah Territory. Said Judge Perrin,

The Victor's Walk

"Here in the capital of the nation, by men full of professions and boastings of loyalty, you have met your first, your only rebuff. . . . Had the so-called rebels torn from the flag twenty-seven bright stars, a Radical Congress would have welcomed the dismantled flag with shouts of joy, as being evidence of an unrepentant people. But it was a rebuke to them to find it pass safely and triumphantly throughout your entire journey without an insult, and requiring no *reconstruction* at their hands."

Bates clambered to the top of the unfinished monument and the folds of Old Glory billowed out in the wind and the rain while hundreds of onlookers raised their voices in tremendous cheers.

During the period of the impeachment proceedings against President Johnson the Northern papers had continued to report that Bates and the flag were received with brass bands and cheering crowds throughout the South. This can only have undermined the Radical Republicans' efforts to further punish the "traitorous Southerners," and how these demonstrations of patriotism influenced the proceedings to impeach Johnson will never be known.

The vote to impeach failed by only a narrow margin, and it never entered the head of the quiet, modest man from Edgerton, Wisconsin, that his march with its overwhelming displays of brotherhood and patriotism may have saved a president.

In any event, Sergeant Bates's star-spangled march showed that—despite past bitter differences between Northerners and Southerners—*they were Americans all.*